From the screen
Co-author of *Never the Bride: a novel*

an inspirational devotional series

volume one
adventures
in faith

cheryl mckay

www.dateswithGod.com
#dateswithGod

Books by Cheryl McKay

Never the Bride: a novel (with Rene Gutteridge)
Finally the Bride: Finding Hope While Waiting
*Finally Fearless: How Overcoming Anxiety Helped Me
Find True Love*
Song of Springhill: a love story
*Spirit of Springhill: Miners, Wives, Widows, Rescuers &
Their Children Tell True Stories of Springhill's Mining
Disasters*
Love's a Stage: a novel (with Rene Gutteridge)
O Little Town of Bethany: a novella (with Rene
Gutteridge)
Greetings from the Flipside a novel (with Rene
Gutteridge)
Wild & Wacky, Totally True Bible Stories Series
(children's books with Frank Peretti)

Films / Videos / Audio Dramas by Cheryl McKay

The Ultimate Gift (screenplay by)
The Ultimate Life (screen story by)
Extraordinary (co-writer)
Indivisible (co-writer)
Gigi: God's Little Princess DVD (screenplay)
Superbook (episode writer)
RiverKids (audio show writer)
Wild & Wacky Totally True Bible Stories Series (audio
show writer)

For Those Who Are Ready
To Embark on a Romantic
Adventure with God

25 DATES WITH GOD:
Volume One
Adventures in Faith

Cover Photo: © ibush - Fotolia.com
Interior Chapter Graphics: © Pavel Sevcov- Fotolia.com
Author Headshot & Morning Glory Photos: © Christopher Price
Cover Design by: Hope River Arts

Please exercise safety and caution when following any of the date
plans in this book. Author and Publisher assume no liability for
activities engaged in by readers of this book.

Published in the United States of America

ISBN-13: 978-1-946344-00-7
ISBN-10: 1-946344-00-1

Copyright © 2016 by Cheryl McKay

First Edition 2016

TABLE OF CONTENTS

1 Peter 1:8-9
"Though you have not seen Him,
you love Him;
and even though you do not see Him now,
you believe in Him and are
filled with an inexpressible and glorious joy,
for you are receiving the end result
of your faith,
the salvation of your souls."

Dating God 101

*D*ear Readers:

Do you know that God, the Creator of the universe wants to go on a date with you? Yes, He is wooing you, summoning you, romancing you with all His heart to go out with Him, at this very moment.

And it starts now. Yes, right now.

That oh-so-very-attractive omnipresent and omniscient thing He has going on allows Him to focus solely on you.

Just you.

Even though I believe everyone—male and female—could benefit from set-aside, private dates with God, I've written this devotional series speaking to the hearts of women. Married or single. However, that doesn't mean that men couldn't benefit from many of the dates in this book.

This volume is called *Adventures in Faith.* It takes faith to believe God will show up and go on a date with you. It takes faith to believe the Almighty is interacting with you, that it's God speaking, holding your hand, and whisking you away into a Divine Romance as only He can.

Dating God takes faith.

If we don't have faith, we may feel silly or feel like we just went out alone. Sisters, we are not alone. God loves us. He craves time alone with *every single one of us.* This applies to whether we have an earthly husband or not.

Regardless of whether you are married or single, how long has it been since you've been on a date? I remained single until I was 39 years old. I went seven years without going on a real date between my last relationship, until that first date with my husband, Chris. So, dates—and what it felt like to go on a real one—were far from my memory for a long time. My husband and I still date, even though we've been married for over five years. However, just because he's by my side doesn't mean I should stop dating God.

Not by a long shot.

If anything, keeping close to the Lover of my Soul, my Savior, and Best Heavenly Friend and Father keeps my marriage stronger. I take care of my marriage by fostering a close relationship with the One who should remain at the center of my life.

And the center of yours.

Remember what it is like to go on a date, to feel those first date flutters? Thankfully, with God, you don't even have to wait until He asks you out, wondering if He likes you enough to spend time with you.

God has already asked you out. His hand is extended toward you. Daily, hourly, minute-by-minute. He aches to spend time with you. If anything, in my own busyness, I've neglected to say "yes" at times.

Now, let's just get one thing out of the way. I'd like to be abundantly clear. When I was single, I hated all those ridiculous comments from well-meaning people. You know the ones:

"Just make Jesus your boyfriend and then maybe God could send you a husband."

If you've read my book for singles called *Finally the Bride*, you know about my journey to the altar and the many reasons people told me why I was still single—and far too long for my taste.

If you are single, please don't read this book as if I'm saying that going on dates with God is how you can earn the right for a husband.

For singles and marrieds alike, this is about your relationship with God, Jesus, and the Holy Spirit. It's about fostering closeness simply for the sake of having a wonderful relationship with the divine members of this Trinity. It's not about your future mate or to improve your relationship with your spouse.

There will be dates worked into this series that will deal with your current or future love relationship, but it's not the focal point. Instead, this book is about fostering intimacy with the God of the universe who desperately wants time with you.

For Him and for you, alone. Not because of anyone else.

A husband will not and cannot replace the Lord. The God who is able to *do* immeasurably more than we ask or imagine (Ephesians 3:20). To *be* more than we ask or imagine.

Each chapter should be its own date with God (Father, Son, and Holy Spirit). Hopefully, the dates will foster closeness, relationship, and communication, all things that help a dating relationship thrive. I hope you enjoy this journey and take your time going through these 25 dates from Volume One of this series.

I have enjoyed going on these dates with God and plan to repeat many. These special times should not be rushed. Instead, use this guide to remind yourself to have consistent time with God. Maybe try one or two a week outside of your regular prayer, Bible reading, and quiet times. Some involve going out; some require staying in.

Before I send you off on Date 1, I want to share a bit about where I got the idea to start a movement called *Dates With God* (#dateswithGod).

God inspired me to write the screenplay for *Never the Bride*. It later became a novel I worked on with novelist, Rene Gutteridge. It will be a movie one day as well. This story sparked the inspiration for this whole book series.

Never the Bride is about a woman in her thirties, Jessie, who accuses God of being asleep on the job of writing her love story. God shows up, in the flesh, to face those charges. (Think *Bruce Almighty*, but God looks younger, handsome, and date-worthy for a thirty-something, frustrated single.)

In this attractive, human form, God tells Jessie if she wants Him to write her love story, she must surrender her pen. The purple pen she's been using her entire life to fill her journals with entries about how she thinks her love life should go. Can she surrender and trust God with that pen? That's the adventure that Jessie embarks on in *Never the Bride*.

At one point, Jessie's birthday approaches. An event that happened for me often when I was single. You know, like once a year. Every year, I battled how to spend my birthday because I never had dates or love interests to spoil me silly on that day. Since it was such a battle for me during my single years, I wanted to put Jessie in that position. (It's only fair that my characters face what I'm forced to go through, right?) When Jessie realizes God is not going to write her love story on time for her 35th birthday like she'd hoped, she's tempted to steal that surrendered purple pen back from Him.

Then, Jessie accepts God's invitation for a date.

I will go into more detail about this date Jessie spends with God in Date 12, titled *Dance With God*. A date where Jessie gets lost in her love for God, dances with Him, and forgets the outside world.

Like Jessie, I invite you to make "dating" part of your love story with God. Go on a journey through the pages to come. Enjoy dates that can create and foster intimacy between you and your Creator. He loves us so much; He wants to spend time with us. He is not distant.

I hope by the end of this book, you know this is true at the deepest parts of your heart and soul.

At the beginning of each date, I will give you a short guideline:

Location:

Supplies:

Reading:

Up front I will let you know what location to choose. Sometimes that may be as simple as "a quiet place." Other times, I'll get specific.

I'll also let you know what supplies to bring, like a journal, a Bible, art supplies, a camera. (Always assume you should bring this book with you, even if sometimes you leave it in the car. I won't include that on the list.) Try to use just one journal for your dates so that notes you take during past dates will be with you.

Some dates will require you to read the chapter in advance. Others you will read the whole chapter during the date. You just need to get to the place with the supplies outlined, then start the chapter once you're settled in at the suggested location.

Here are a few additional guidelines. When experiencing these dates with God, I encourage you to set aside electronics that aren't specifically needed for the date. For safety, when away from home, bring your phone. Maybe use airplane mode or silent mode and keep it out of sight.

Spend time with the One you're with, not letting the outside world distract you. Treat God as you *should* treat a human date. For example, not letting your phone pull your attention from Him.

You will often need a camera, which tends to be our phones. Try to make sure you're not checking email, Facebook, Pinterest, Instagram, or texting and taking calls during your set-apart time with God.

I'd love for you to take selfies or photos of things God shows you while out on dates. These photos will tie into a future date. Plus, I want you to have something to share with the rest of us if you choose to participate through the hashtag:

#dateswithGod

If you use Twitter, also tag our handle: @purplepenworks.

To join the fun, share pictures, insights, or anything you want about God encountering or encouraging you on these dates.

I want you recording memories, moments, words said between yourself and God in the journal you use for this dating relationship. Yes, I do mean that. Expect two-way communication. If you feel like the Holy Spirit speaks something to your heart, write it down. Capture your memories together.

The first two dates are foundational to the rest of the dates. They may not be the most "romantic" of this set of 25. I ask for your patience, to bear with me and not skip ahead to "the good stuff." The dates to come will be that much better because of the time you spend setting a good foundation for your dating relationship with God in those first two dates.

Ready to venture into your heavenly romance? Let's move on to Date 1.

Date 1
The DTR

Location: A quiet place at home.
Supplies: A journal.
Reading: Read chapter during your date.

$\mathcal{T}$his first date is called *The DTR* (a.k.a. Define the Relationship).

The Who, What, Where, When, and Why Date.

As women, we love to know what's going on in relationships, especially of the dating variety. Yet, sometimes it's awkward to broach the topic. Well, guess what? With God, you have permission. Even on this first date.

Can you imagine what would happen if you were on a first date with a potential new beau, in the flesh, and asked, "Can we define this? What are we?

Where is this going? Are we getting married in six months? How many children are we having?" You'd probably send the guy running away scared.

God, on the other hand, is not afraid of your questions. He's not afraid to help you define the most romantic relationship you can ever be in.

Yours and His.

You already have a relationship with Him. If you show up and want to ask questions or share your heart with Him, God has a "bring it on" attitude. He loves communicating with you. Going through these segments of the DTR, He gets your time and attention.

In case you didn't know, He really loves your company. So dive in.

The Who

Just so we are clear, this book is about the God of the Bible. (God, Jesus, and the Holy Spirit.) That's it. No one else. We'll get deeper into more specifics about "Who God is to you" on a future date. For now, journal how you feel about God at this moment. Even if you're struggling — with faith, with emotions, with disappointments — tell Him.

Honesty is a desirable trait in a strong dating relationship. So get honest with God! Write it out. Do you feel like you aren't as in love with Him as you should be, or in love with Him at all? When "Defining God," do you see Him as distant and remote? That is something we want to work on through this dating relationship. Write what you feel about Him right now so we have a starting place.

Share your heart. Hopefully, any challenges you pinpoint now will improve by the end of the first 25 dates. Even if you're starting out in a good place, my hope is that you'll be even closer by Date 25 when we double back to look at this journal entry.

Next, look at God as a suitor. What does that mean to you? Think of God as someone who is calling you for dates with Him. How does it make you feel to ponder that He wants this focused, private time with you?

The What

Now that you know "who" you're dating, think about what you hope this relationship becomes. Tell Him where you're hoping to be after these 25 intimate dates with Him, even if you're not there right now. What kind of growth do you hope for?

You will reap benefits by setting aside specific amounts of time to spend with just Him, without distraction. It may take a few dates to feel it. But trust me — it will come.

To help you with this part of the journal entry, let's try a little exercise.

Make a list of what you feel makes a good date. With that handsome, in-the-flesh, human. That list can translate to your dating relationship with God. I can get you started with part of my list, but feel free to add your own items:

Hallmarks of a Good Date:
- Communication / Conversation
- Sharing / Giving
- Getting to know each other better
- Finding out something new and fresh you didn't already know about the person
- Romance
- Having fun and laughing, sharing a good sense of humor
- Feeling like you've been paid attention to, listened to, and prioritized
- Doing something you both enjoy
- Alternatively, sacrificing your comfort zone for the sake of the other, doing something your date enjoys
- Creating good memories
- Capturing those memories in photos or a journal

What else would you add to this list? Write it down so you can define for God what you'd be looking for in a good dating relationship with Him and what you would enjoy.

Try to remember, this is about both of you and should be mutually beneficial. It's not just about "what can God do for me." It's also not about a removed God who only wants something from you. He craves intimacy with you as well and would be happy to see you plan dates around what *you* enjoy, too.

These hallmarks of a good, in-person date should translate well to how we'd like to be treated by God. Plus, how we hope to treat Him, or how He'd like to be treated.

Use this list as a guide for all future dates.

Write it out as a prayer. This date entry is one you're going to revisit at the end of this book, so you can see where you started to where you end up. Make sure you label it Date 1 so you can find it later. It will be so neat by Date 25 to be able to look back and see how far you've grown since this journey began.

The Where

For some dates, the locations will be specified outside of your home. For this date, examine your home surroundings.

Pinpoint your favorite spots in and around your home. Where do you get the most privacy, the least interruption? Do you have a chair on your front porch or back patio or both? Do you have a bedroom you can slip into, even a spare one? A kitchen table or couch at 5 a.m. when no one else is awake? A closet?

I like variety *and* privacy. (I have four favorite

spots in my home for quiet times.) Just make sure it's quiet and comfortable. Keep all of those places in mind for any home-based dates in the future. For dates outside the home, I'll suggest what to look for.

The When
Make appointments. Take out a calendar. Set aside specific times, at least once a week, when you'll go on a date with God. This is in addition to your regular Bible reading or prayer times. Some require field trips out. Put God on the calendar in the same way you'd put a guy on there (for a date with a boyfriend or husband). Try your best to stick to the schedule.

Don't be one of those chronic date cancelers. Remember that God will be expecting you, and that nobody likes to be stood up.

The Why
Evaluate what made you get this book. Why do you feel spending time with God in a dating relationship will be good for both of you? Tell God why you want to date Him. Then ask Him, "Why would You like to date me?" See if He whispers something to your heart. If so, write it down.

Here's a prayer answer I jotted down—from God—when I asked Him this same question:

"I crave intimacy with you, just like you

crave intimacy from relationships. Focus on Me and spend time with Me. I miss you when we don't spend time together. Pursue Me as if you were pursuing your long-term relationship. We grow apart when we don't spend time together, just like you would in a dating relationship whether dating a potential mate or your husband. Good relationships need communication. Let's sup together, fellowship, and commune."

Hear me, Dear Sisters. God loves *you*. He wants time with you; He wants to speak to you. Dine with you. Dance with you. He doesn't want you to live vicariously through others and their relationships with Him.

Don't be like the Israelites who insisted Moses talk to God instead of talking to God themselves (Exodus 20:18-19). This time is about you and your personal relationship with God.

So this was only the first date, where going deep was welcomed right away. You got right down to business with The DTR.

Are you ready to grow in intimacy with God? Are you ready to date the One who created romance, intimacy, and designed us for relationship with Him? He's waiting and available, as often as you will accept His hand.

Date 2
Clear the Air

Location: A quiet place at home.
Supplies: A journal.
Reading: Read chapter during your date.

I know what you're thinking: how can a date titled "Clear the Air" be fun, let alone romantic? Didn't I buy this book for the romance? For the good times?

Well, yes. You did. And that's my motive in writing it. However, this is one of those dates we must have near the beginning of this *Dates With God* journey so the rest of your dates can be that much better. So please. Don't skip it. I promise. They get a lot more fun. Since this is extremely private, try to have this date at home.

Have you ever been on a date with someone when there was *something* between you? Meaning, some unresolved issue or conflict? It's not the most fun, is it? That elephant in the room that needs addressing. You're in a restaurant or at a park or some place that is supposed to be enjoyable. You don't want to be the killjoy that messes up the night.

However, leaving the needed conversation unspoken, are you still enjoying yourself? Does leaving the issue between you in limbo help you relax into the date? No. If only you could clear the air first, then the rest of the night could be a blast, right? Usually, yes. Especially when you have a date who is on your side and wants to work through conflicts, not create them.

With God, you don't have to ask when the right time is to come clean and apologize and ask for forgiveness. His door is always open for repentance and offering forgiveness or just plain clearing the air. Even on a date. It won't harm your fun with Him. In fact, it will strengthen your relationship, once you get whatever that is out of the way.

To fully fellowship with you, God needs this clean air. You need this, too.

> Isaiah 59:2
> "But your iniquities have separated you from your God; your sins have hidden His face from you, so that He will not hear."

This particular date is early on in your *Dates*

With God journey on purpose because I want you get that slate wiped clean. You can always revisit this date again later if something new comes up—and it will. We're fallen beings who make mistakes. We sin on a regular basis. Any time in the future, you can repeat the practice yourself.

The Bible is clear. Those of us who accept Jesus as Lord and Savior are forgiven. Yet we still need to go through the practice of asking for forgiveness and receiving that forgiveness offered graciously to us by God Himself.

Looking at the Slate
Has anything happened lately that you know has grieved God's heart? Is there an area of disobedience standing between you? This could be an isolated incident. It could be a habitual sin that may need some work to remove.

God hates sin, not the sinner. It's hard for Him to be around the sin itself. So how about we do Him and us a favor and allow Him to help us eradicate it?

Even though this may not sound like the most fun date of this book, it's an important one to take care of early on so the rest of your dates can be as enjoyable as possible. I don't want anything standing between you and God and hearing His voice. Sin will affect your hearing and fellowship.

We may like to ignore this one, but there is a verse that talks about how God responds to those who turn a "deaf ear" to Him and choose to live in disobedience.

> Proverbs 28:9
> "If anyone turns a deaf ear to My instruction, even his prayers are detestable."

Does that sound a bit harsh? It's in the Bible. People today like to talk about the loving and forgiving side of Jesus, but toss away and forget the "Go and sin no more" part of Jesus (John 8:11). Out of His great love for us, He doesn't want us to keep wallowing in the same sins. He knows they aren't good for us.

I don't know about you, but I do not want my Heavenly Date to find my chatter detestable. I'm sensitive about whether or not I am listened to. In fact, early on in a dating relationship, if a man wasn't a good listener, he quickly got crossed off my list as a potential, lifelong mate. (Chris happens to be a wonderful listener, thankfully.)

I want God to hear me, to listen, to chat back with me, to interact. But when sin stands between us, we need to clear that up first.

So, come on. Let's do it!

If you've ever doubted whether or not you can hear God's voice, one easy way to get an answer—and quickly—is to ask these questions:

Lord, is there anything standing between You and me? Do I have any sins I haven't confessed to You?

I feel sure—if there is anything—the Holy Spirit will quickly light it up on your mind. He'll remind you of something (or somethings) you need to confess, areas you need to make changes, especially in habitual sin.

We are forgiven. Jesus already took care of our sins on the cross, when we accepted Him as Lord and Savior. However, that doesn't mean that sinful behavior won't drive a wedge between us going forward. That verse in Proverbs is clear enough.

Think about it like a marriage. You've taken vows. You've promised to stay together till death do you part. Does that mean you would willingly offend that spouse over and again just because they've promised to stay? Not if you want a good marriage.

As hard as it may be to admit that sticking point between you and God, use this date to write down what the Holy Spirit reveals. If there's anything big that would take some work to get rid of, ask Him to help you with an action plan. He's here to love you through it, and to help you overcome sin.

1 John 1:9
"If we confess our sins, He is faithful and just and will forgive us our sins and purify us from all unrighteousness."

1 Corinthians 10:13

"No temptation has overtaken you except what is common to mankind. And God is faithful; He will not let you be tempted beyond what you can bear. But when you are tempted, He will also provide a way out so that you can endure it."

Today's Sin

What areas do you struggle to remain in a place of righteousness?

Because of the influence of our current society, it may not hurt to go straight back to the Bible and remind yourself what God considers sin. Culture has tried so hard to redefine sin and tell us what is right and wrong. Many have forgotten to go back to the Word, to go back to what God has to say about the matter. Culture and society do not determine what is or is not sin. Neither do I. The Lord does.

Jesus is the same yesterday, today, and forever (Hebrews 13:8). He hasn't changed His mind about what sins grieve His heart and what separates us from *fellowship* with Him.

So use this date to go back to the Bible. Look up the lists of sins available. See if there's anything in there the Holy Spirit will show you.

I'll give you a short list of Old and New Testament passages to get you started, but don't stop there. Do your own search of God's Word or ask the

Holy Spirit if there are particular passages you should take a look at.

Time to dive in the deep end. Start with the following passages:

- Exodus 20:1-17
- Romans 1:24-32
- Galatians 5:13-26
- Ephesians 5:1-20

If something in those passages bothers you — behaviors you don't want to believe are sinful — understand that I am not the author of the Bible. I didn't write those lists of what grieves God's heart. I can't change or rewrite what God has said. The best action you can take is to share your feelings with God. Give Him the opportunity to talk to you about it. Ask Him to help you understand why He has those boundaries in place and why He believes it's for your best.

Let's just admit it. Sometimes the Bible doesn't tell us what we want to hear. It goes against our flesh and what it desires.

Jesus distilled the Ten Commandments down to two key commands: Love God first and love your neighbor. However, Jesus was not saying that nothing else was sin. Also, He wasn't saying that loving your neighbor means telling them that whatever *feels right* to them is good. I'll quote the portion of Scripture this comes from. You'll notice in context, Jesus was asked a question about which commandment is greatest:

> Matthew 22: 36-40
> "Teacher, which is the greatest commandment in the Law?" 37 Jesus replied: "'Love the LORD your God with all your heart and with all your soul and with all your mind.' 38 This is the first and greatest commandment. 39 And the second is like it: 'Love your neighbor as yourself.' 40 All the Law and the Prophets hang on these two commandments."

Notice, Jesus highlights the commands in answer to the question. He wasn't saying the rest of the commandments don't matter. He was saying a love of God and a love of people will help you follow the rest of the list. For example, if you love your neighbors, you're not stealing from them, murdering them, burning in jealousy over their blessings, or having affairs with their spouses.

It sincerely grieves my heart to think of what it must be like right now for young people to enter the dating world. They live in a world that tells them sex before marriage is acceptable, attempting to imply it's no longer a sin or even abnormal to wait. That it's not harmful, that God doesn't care anymore.

This is absolutely false.

It's a lie straight from the pit of Hell. God hasn't changed. He designed marriage for a purpose and sex to be within that safe, covenant relationship.

If you've let society convince you otherwise, engaging in that habitual sin will harm your fellowship with God, your ability to hear His still small voice.

Just because society or that cute "Christian" man at church acts like sex before marriage isn't wrong anymore—and even encourages multiple partners—doesn't mean that it is not a sin. It truly is damaging to you, your emotional health, your relationship with God, and to your future marriage.

That's just one sin example. There are many others. I bring that specific one up since it's so closely tied to our dating lives.

I've counseled many women grieved that God hasn't allowed them to get married so far in life. Yet, they sleep around on any date they get. It hurts my heart.

For them and for God.

God gets blamed for something that has nothing to do with Him. He hurts for these women as well. They will not find what they are aching to find this way.

As you do a check-in today of possible sins between you and God, be brave. Ask the Holy Spirit to help you see the truth. Ask Him to help you see if you are guilty of any of these areas, regardless of what society, peers, or your family tells you.

Once that slate is cleaned, by asking for forgiveness and then repenting (which also means *turning* from your sin), your intimate times with God will be revolutionized. It will be over, done, and the guilt wiped away. We may not always escape consequences of past behavior. But our guilt is gone, and we are now free!

The wall between you and God will be torn down. The rest of these dates will be that much more fun, intimate, and beautiful.

Journey on in this love relationship, basking in that newfound freedom. Take a deep breath of that fresh, cleaned air.

Date 3
Who is God to Me?

Location: A quiet place, preferably outside, like a park
bench or picnic table.

Supplies: A journal, a Bible, Internet connection (ex.
through a phone or tablet).

Reading: Read chapter during your date.

You should know who you're dating, right? (Or
married to.)

Part of dating is getting to know the person.
Even after marriage, you continue to get to know
your spouse every day on a deeper level. But it helps
to know something about the person when you go
on those early dates. Conversation starters, tidbits.

Thankfully, one way to know God is to read His
autobiography—that Book He inspired people to

write about Him. *The Bible*.

Don't worry. I won't ask you to read the whole Bible on one date. I'll even let you use your phone or tablet to search the Internet for information about Him. (Admit it: you probably Facebook stalked—I mean, researched—a date or your future spouse online, right?)

I want you to search "Names of God." Find sites that list various names from Scripture for God, Jesus, and the Holy Spirit. Read the verses the names come from.

Make a list in your journal of your favorite ones, those that feel familiar to you. Then make a list of those that reflect a part of God you would like to get to know better.

Do this exercise first, then I will share some of my favorite examples. Take your time. There are over 100 names for our Lord in the Bible, all reflecting different parts of His personality worth getting to know.

Now I'd like to share some of my favorite verses that supply names or personalities of our beloved Trinity.

Here are just a few of the names I love for God:

Father (1 Corinthians 8:6, Psalm 68:5)
Jehovah Jirah – Provider (Genesis 22:14)
Deliverer (Psalm 18:2)

Check out this verse with four names for Jesus:

Isaiah 9:6:
"For to us a child is born, to us a Son is given, and the government will be on His shoulders. And He will be called Wonderful Counselor, Mighty God, Everlasting Father, Prince of Peace."

Do know Jesus as your Wonderful Counselor or Prince of Peace? Those are two of my favorites to call upon when I'm in need of His help or peace.

I love that Jesus also names us His friends (John 15:15). (We certainly want to be friends with the One we are dating, right?)

Jesus is revealed countless times in Scripture as the Healer. (That's another part of Him I seem to need a lot!)

Then we have the Holy Spirit. In John 14:16-17, Jesus promised the Holy Spirit to His people:

"And I will ask the Father, and He will give you another Advocate to help you and be with you forever— the Spirit of Truth. The world cannot accept Him, because it neither sees Him nor knows Him. But you know Him, for He lives with you and will be in you."

In this passage, the Holy Spirit is called Advocate and Spirit of Truth. The word Advocate has also been translated as "Comforter."

Because there are many names for God, Jesus, and the Holy Spirit throughout His Word, they collectively have personalities for anything we'd ever need. (Thankfully, this is not the scary, split personality of Jekyll and Hyde you could encounter on a bad date.)

As you continue on this dating journey, keep an eye on ways God may reveal Himself to you over the course of your dates. Especially in the ways you have asked God to show Himself.

For example, are you struggling with provision? Ask God to show Himself to you as Provider (Jehovah Jireh). Did you have a rough experience with your earthly father, which has tainted your ability to believe God can be a good Father? Ask God to heal that by showing you He's a good Father.

Have you had trouble following the right path? Ask Jesus to show Himself to you as the Good Shepherd.

Do you need a healing, emotionally or physically? Call upon Jehovah Rapha, our Great Physician and Healer.

I firmly believe the Lord will show Himself to you in ways you seek Him.

Naturally, this all comes down to getting to know our Heavenly Father. To know Him, we need to spend time with Him. We need to know and recognize His voice. It starts with Scripture and continues with our prayer life.

There is no way around it. Time is a worthy investment. Just like when getting to know someone we're dating or our spouses, you can't do that if you don't spend time with the person. The same is true of God.

Getting to know God and all of His "personalities" and the ways He's likely to relate to us is a great way to start.

Date 4
How Do I Love Thee?

Location: A quiet place at home, at a table.

Supplies: A journal *or* colored index cards, scissors, and a decorative, wooden box.

Reading: Read chapter during your date.

$\mathcal{W}$hen someone loves you, it's nice to know why. Doesn't it help when they're willing to stop, take time to share with you everything they love about you, putting it into specifics? Actual words?

Words of affirmation is a love language highlighted in Gary Chapman's book called *The Five Love Languages*. My husband and I have this funny joke where after one of us says something nice to the other, the receiver of that compliment says, "Shower me with compliments." The person continues with other affirmations. We may be a bit sappy at times, but we love hearing it.

So does God.

God longs to hear why we love Him too. It's why He suggests praising Him. Singing songs to Him. When talking to God, He loves when we don't just make it a time of asking for our own needs.

Can you imagine if you were in a relationship and your boyfriend only chose to speak to you when he wanted something from you? Wouldn't that hurt? Wouldn't it feel one-sided? We don't want to make God feel that way, either.

God wants to be sought out because of our love for Him and not just what He can do for us. He wants us to spend time with Him because we love Him. Not just to see His hand and His works and His power.

Just take a moment to think about how hollow you'd feel in a relationship with someone who only wanted you for selfish needs. Naturally, I don't mean we can't pray for our needs; we absolutely should. That will even become part of other date activities in this book series. The focus of this date is to turn our love and praise toward God. Let's give Him a chance to enjoy our affections and love for Him without an agenda.

There was a song they used to sing at my church in the 1990s that had a lyric about how a rock wasn't going to stand in the place of a person who wanted to praise God. It was talking about the verses in Luke 19:38-40 about how if the people didn't praise God, the rocks would cry out instead. Our pastor declared no rock would praise God instead of him. I've never forgotten that sermon.

God will be praised, one way or the other. Do you want to be part of that? A part of making Him feel loved, appreciated, desired, simply because of who He is and how wonderful He is?

Or would you rather He have to listen to a rock?

Let's first take a look at Scripture. These are just a few segments from Psalms that talk about Praising God. There are countless others.

Psalm 100
Shout for joy to the LORD, all the earth. 2 Worship the LORD with gladness; come before Him with joyful songs. 3 Know that the LORD is God. It is He who made us, and

we are His; we are His people, the sheep of His pasture. 4 Enter His gates with thanksgiving and His courts with praise; give thanks to Him and praise His name. 5 For the LORD is good and His love endures forever; His faithfulness continues through all generations.

Psalm 95:1-7

Come, let us sing for joy to the LORD; let us shout aloud to the Rock of our salvation. 2 Let us come before Him with thanksgiving and extol Him with music and song. 3 For the LORD is the great God, the great King above all gods. 4 In His hand are the depths of the earth, and the mountain peaks belong to Him. 5 The sea is His, for He made it, and His hands formed the dry land. 6 Come, let us bow down in worship, let us kneel before the LORD our Maker; 7 for He is our God and we are the people of His pasture, the flock under His care. Today, if only you would hear His voice.

Psalm 150

Praise the LORD. Praise God in His sanctuary; praise Him in His mighty heavens. 2 Praise Him for His acts of power; praise Him for His surpassing greatness. 3 Praise Him with the sounding of the trumpet, praise Him with the harp and lyre, 4 praise Him with timbrel and dancing, praise Him with the strings and pipe, 5 praise Him with the clash of cymbals, praise Him with resounding cymbals. 6 Let everything that has breath praise the LORD. Praise the LORD.

One object that does not have breath is a rock. And yet, if God isn't praised, He'll cause those rocks to praise Him. That tells you how important praise is to Him.

Love in Technicolor
For today's date, I'd like to suggest you use something other than a journal. This gets into a craft project. When I did this, I cut up little colored index cards into pieces long enough to write one sentence. I asked myself, "Why do I love God?" I wrote out one trait or comment on each card. These answers stemmed from answered prayers, to Names of God that express attributes I've come to love, to just praising Him for what I love about Him.

I then put these answers in a decorative box that I can take out and reread any time I want to remind myself of His goodness.

If the craft side of this assignment sounds like too much trouble, feel free to just write out a list in a journal. But for the artsy types, feel free to make this like a gift for God. (I made one for my husband as well for one of our anniversaries.)

To help get you started, I'll share a few examples from my cards about God:

How Do I Love Thee

You sent Your Son to die for me.

You saved me.

You provide for me.

You offer grace in difficult circumstances.

You never slumber.

You watch over me.

You hug me when I'm lonely.

You wink at me.

You listen to me.

You let me cry out to You when I'm sad.

You take walks with me.

You see the big picture of my life.

You have my best interests in mind.

You've guided me away from making mistakes.

You've forgiven me for the ones I have made.

You talk to me.

You make me laugh.

You have a great sense of humor.

You know how to Romans 8:28 my life. You turn all things around for good.

You open doors for me no man can shut.

You've allowed me to do what I love for a
living: to write.

You love spending time with me.

You meet me where I'm at. If I'm having a bad
day, you accept me as is.

You love me.

So those are a few examples of the phrases I
wrote out for God as my way of praising Him. I'm
sure we'll have some things in common, plus you'll
have unique things for your list. Take your time with
this. Shower God with the compliments He aches to
hear from you. Write them down and then read
them out loud like a prayer to Him.

Once you finish, go back and reread those
Psalms I quoted and see if those mention attributes
of God worthy of praise that you may have forgotten
to write down. Read other parts of Scripture for
reasons to praise Him.

This special box or list doesn't need to be
completed in one sitting. Use this date to start it. (If
you decide to make a decorative box of these, feel
free to post a picture and hashtag it so we can see
what you came up with.)

Throughout your dating life with God, you can
add to this box. I imagine as these dates with Him
continue, you'll think of more compliments to add.

This is because our God and His love for us are
boundless. If you keep your eyes open, you will see

the wonderful ways in which He loves you.

On our next date, we're going to take the time to reverse this assignment. We are going to allow God to tell you the reasons why He loves *you*.

Date 5
How God Loves You

Location: A quiet place, a romantic setting. Preferably outside, like a park or garden, ocean or mountain area.

Supplies: A journal and a Bible.

Reading: Read chapter during your date.

*T*here was a painful time in my life when I thought I was getting married. This man told me the reason we had to break up was that he didn't love me. He'd prayed for God to "make me a treasure to him" so that he could fall in love with me, but God didn't do it.

You know the verse: "For where your treasure is, there your heart will be also" (Matthew 6:21). Apparently, God wasn't interested in making me a treasure to this man or allowing him to fall in love with me.

Have you ever had to recover from such a painful blow? For me to hear "I don't love you" and "You are not a treasure" pierced my fragile heart.

Those words took me the longest to get over. I feel like God had to go into overtime hours for months to heal me from the erroneous beliefs I adopted. I told myself, "Cheryl, you are not a treasure. You are unlovable."

God feels the exact opposite about me than this man did. But when I was in a place of loneliness and pain — and I desperately wanted to be married — it was hard to accept God's love.

Even though the eight months that followed that break up were eight of the most painful ones of my life, God showed up in mighty ways to love me, care for me, tend to me, and heal me. Heal me of depression, of erroneous beliefs I'd held about myself and my lovability.

In hindsight, I know without a doubt that God rescued me from the wrong person and a lifetime of heartache. God was saving me for my real husband. I'd have to wait for Chris. I went dateless for seven years after that horrific break up until God let me go out on that first date with Chris.

Well, except, pivotal dates with God of course.

So, what did God do with me in the meantime? He showered me with love and affection. I couldn't always accept it. Yet there were times He'd break through and do something so awesome that I knew He was saying something like, "I love you, Cheryl, let me count the ways."

I want to show you a couple of examples. While I share a lot more about this healing journey in my book *Finally Fearless*, I want to include an excerpt here:

> Around the time of the breakup, two people came to me separately with messages from God. I hadn't told either of them what was said to me regarding a treasure. One message was the verse Proverbs 3:15, which says, "She is more precious than rubies; nothing you desire can compare with her." While that verse refers to wisdom, I believe God pulled out the isolated verse just for me.
>
> The other person came to me and said she saw a vision God told her was for me. It was of God with rubies in His hand, considering them as though they were precious to Him.
>
> Both of these words, I believe, were God's attempt to heal me right away from the arrows of my ex-boyfriend's words. However, it was too close to the time I'd

received the blow; I didn't let God's words sink into my heart. In fact, I hadn't even noticed the connection between rubies and a treasure until much later when I had gone back through my journals and realized what God had tried to do for me.

Sometime later, when I was still healing from all this, I was sitting at the beach in Santa Monica with a trusted friend, one who counseled me through much of the depression. I was starting to peek out from the darkness but still needed some encouragement.

Suddenly, my cell phone rang. I answered it. The caller asked for "Ruby." I told him he had the wrong number. When I hung up, my friend and I looked at each other and chuckled. Did God just allow that person to call my phone accidentally to remind me I am His treasure? It felt like a little kiss from Heaven. Many people dismiss these as coincidences. I call them GodWinks. (Long before I'd heard of SQuire Rushnell's amazing *GodWinks* book series.)

From these stories, you may see God speaking to me about why He loved me, reminding me of three things:

- I'm a treasure.
- I am His Ruby.
- I am lovable.

Those were affirmations I needed to hear from God. I wasn't hearing them from an earthly relationship with a man. Quite the opposite.

Another time I was feeling unlovable, God encouraged me to look up the meaning of my name.

Cheryl means *Beloved*.

The moment was just another sweet reminder of how God sees me, which is much more important than how a man or any family member sees me.

Your Turn

So, how about you? Are you in need of some affirmation, a sense of why God loves you? As you now sit in whatever quiet place you've chosen, will you allow Him to speak to you about this?

We are going to do this in two ways. First through God's Word, then through His still small voice.

I'll kick this off with some verses about God's love for us. I'd like you to extract reasons He loves you or what He's done to show you His love from these verses. As you read each one, make a list of what you spot in these verses about God and how much He loves you.

John 3:16
"For God so loved the world that He gave His one and only Son, that whoever believes in Him shall not perish but have eternal life."

Zephaniah 3:17

"The LORD your God is with you, the Mighty Warrior who saves. He will take great delight in you; in His love He will no longer rebuke you, but will rejoice over you with singing."

Romans 8:38-39

"For I am convinced that neither death nor life, neither angels nor demons, neither the present nor the future, nor any powers, neither height nor depth, nor anything else in all creation, will be able to separate us from the love of God that is in Christ Jesus our LORD."

Psalm 86:15

"But You, LORD, are a compassionate and gracious God, slow to anger, abounding in love and faithfulness."

1 John 3:1

"See what great love the Father has lavished on us, that we should be called children of God! And that is what we are! The reason the world does not know us is that it did not know Him."

I'm sure you spotted more in these verses than I'll list. Here are some of my favorite points:

- He sent His only Son to die for us.
- God takes delight in us. I really like that He loves us out of delight. Not obligation.
- I love that He "rejoices over us with singing." How cool is that?
- Nothing can separate us from His love.
- He calls us His children; we're His family.

There are many more treasures about God's love for us in His Word. This barely scratches the surface.

Hear me, Sisters. He does love you. No matter what anyone else tells you about your lovability, God's love never fails us.

Now it's your turn.

I encourage you to spend time looking for additional verses from His Word. Find clues that tell you why He loves you so much.

When you spot verses that explain His love for you, keep adding to your list. This list can be vital during times when you're feeling lonely or in need of encouragement. You can refer to it any time.

Ask Him to reveal to you, specifically, why He loves you as His unique daughter.

If you're not used to listening for God's whisper — His still, small voice — this exercise may be a stretch for you. But trust that He loves you and wants to tell you specific reasons why.

For the next part of this date, set your journal open next to you, and ask God a question:

Lord, what do You love about me?

Sit. Be patient. Wait for God's still small, affirming voice. Have a pen ready. (If you're like me, it'll be a purple pen.) Write down anything you feel God says personally to you about why He loves you.

So, how did that feel? Did you enjoy listening to God shower you with His unending love? Now that you're done, I'll share an example of how I feel God answered when I asked, "Why do You love me?"

Why Do You Love Me?
You love My Son.
You accept My Son.
You believe Me.
You have the gift of faith to believe Me even when conventional wisdom says you shouldn't.
You speak about Me to others.
You are My treasure. My ruby.

You share your stories to help draw others to
    Me.
You enjoy writing projects in My Name.
You care about the sanctity of marriage.
I love that you care about purity.
I love you like Christ loves the church.
I love when you want to spend time with Me.

Any time you're feeling down or lonely, go back
to the entry you wrote during this date and reread it.
Remind yourself of all the reasons God loves you.

I hope your ears are getting sensitive to God's voice,
either in His still, small voice inside your heart, or
through the Holy Scriptures as they reveal why God
loves you so much. Write them down each time God
lights up something on your heart and mind. Keep
that treasure of a list to go back to or add to any
time.

Date 6
Prayer Walks

Location: Your neighborhood or a neighboring one.
Supplies: A phone to record or text yourself notes, if
    needed.
Reading: Read whole chapter before your date.

In 2003, when I went through the darkest year of
my life, I started a tradition with God called Prayer
Walks. It was a terrific way to get out of the house,
away from the computer (especially before Smart
Phones). I could enjoy nature or neighborhoods or
wherever I wanted to walk that day.

On any date—even today—one of my favorite
things to do is just take a walk and hold hands. As
long as I have my husband by my side, holding my
hand, I am entertained. I don't need him to spend

lavish amounts of money on me, take me to fancy restaurants. Just a walk on the beach, a walk through a nice neighborhood to look at unique or pretty architecture or a park is entertaining enough.

Back in 2003, the more I went on these walks with God — which felt like going on dates — the hungrier I got to take them. They became almost a daily event, an appointment with God I couldn't wait to keep.

Sometimes, even if it were raining, I'd throw on a raincoat and go anyway. I didn't want to miss these precious moments with God.

I used the time to pray, either for specific needs or to praise Him for what He was doing in my life to heal me from all the pain. To share my heart with Him, even when I was angry or frustrated or hurt.

I'd pray "in the Spirit" if I didn't know how to pray (Romans 8:26). I did a lot of that. It really calmed my soul to pray that way and assume the Holy Spirit would take over and pray correctly. For example, I'd feel impressed to pray for a particular person, not knowing what was going on, and ask the Holy Spirit to take over and intercede of their behalf.

Those prayer walks were precious. They continued almost daily for about 2 years. I still go on them a couple times a week.

As you are about to embark on this practice of Prayer Walk Dates, make a list of possible locations for this one and future ones.

Where close by would be good to go? Your own neighborhood? If you live in a neighborhood where it's the time of day you can be free from distraction or running into a ton of neighbors—great! If you think you'll get interrupted a lot—because you are the social butterfly everyone knows—head to another neighborhood where people don't know you.

I always enjoy seeing new architecture and roaming outside my own neighborhood. So I like to do both. Plus, as you go on more walks, you'll want the variety.

Is there a destination you can walk to? A nearby park? Can you visit a botanical garden? Or go on a mountain hike? What do you have access to that would allow you to plan these dates? We currently have many different ways I can walk in our neighborhood.

Prayer walks shouldn't be for only one date. They should become a regular practice, a standing date you share with God.

Some of these locations I'll suggest as part of other dates in this book. In general I'd like you to start making a list of safe places you can go regularly to enjoy these walks with God.

Give yourself at least 30 minutes, more if you have it. There's something romantic about a good stroll, particularly in the golden time of the morning or late afternoon.

During your walk, talk to God. Invite Him to talk to you. If you sense He is talking, try to record it into your phone for later transcribing.

If God speaks to me while I'm out, I speak-text it into my phone to my email. Then later I cut and paste from the email into a journal document on my computer. I like to save everything I feel God says. Sometimes, it's great to look back on it. Especially if God speaks about something that hasn't happened yet.

Historically, before Smart Phones, I would bring old-fashioned paper and pen. I was spotted more than once sitting on some random person's curb, writing down something important. (They had no idea God was talking to me. I probably just looked like a typical, Hollywood screenwriter, getting a new brainstorm that just couldn't wait until I got home.)

If you doubt whether God wants to speak to you today, I encourage you to read *4 Keys to Hearing God's Voice* by Mark and Patti Virkler of Communion with God ministries. It details how to hear then write down what you hear in journals. It's the book that got me started in that practice (under its former title *Dialogue With God*). Every journal date is a date with God.

Give Prayer Walk Dates a try. I promise. As you start to encounter Him when you're out, your hunger for these walks will become insatiable. You won't be able to resist going on more walks, and you'll look forward to each one. I know that's what happened to me. Especially the more I sensed His tangible presence. I got addicted to spending time with Him — and that's a good addiction.

In the next chapter, I'll get more specific with a type of Prayer Walk date that you may want to incorporate on many occasions. But first, just keep it simple and go on that first Prayer Walk now. What are you waiting for?

Date 7
Here's Winking at You, Kid

Location: Your neighborhood or a neighboring one.

Supplies: A phone to record or text yourself notes, and a camera.

Reading: Read whole chapter before your date.

𝓛et's take "Prayer Walks" a step further and move into one where you keep your eyes open for GodWinks.

My buddy, SQuire Rushnell, has a book series out about *GodWinks*. Long before I had ever heard of him and his lovely wife, Louise Duart, I had named these precious moments with the Lord "GodWinks." Those moments when I felt like He'd show me something meaningful or cute or even funny.

Later, I found out there was a whole book series

by Rushnell filled with these types of stories.

Today, I want to get you out of the house and looking for GodWinks during your walk with God.

For this one, take God and your camera. This way, if you do have any special encounters, you can photograph it. Consider sharing your photos online with the hashtag:

#dateswithGod

So what's a GodWink? I asked God to encounter me on these Prayer Walks in some tangible way. Sometimes, He'd show me symbols from a dream I'd had the night before, something I couldn't have manufactured on my own. I felt like it was His way of saying "hi" to His daughter. (That's me!)

Other times, there would be a message on a license plate or bumper sticker that had special meaning for me.

Or I'd ask to see something in particular. The times when He actually would do it blew my proverbial socks off. It didn't happen every time, but when it did, it was obvious God showed up to say "hi" or wink or wave or smile or make me laugh.

Let me share a few stories with you first so you have an idea of what a date looks like when God winks at you.

GodWink Samples

One day, when going out on a walk, I needed to stop by the grocery store first to drop off three bags of cans for recycling and get some money back. I prayed: "Lord, if you allow someone to come across my path that I can bless with these cans so they can take the money instead, I'd love to do that." Then I prayed, "How about the person I've seen a couple of times with a shopping cart that works so hard to collect cans from people's trash?"

As I walked down the sidewalk from my Studio City apartment, I rounded the corner and guess who I see? That exact person with their shopping cart, looking for cans. I walked up to them and said, "Would you like these?" They just smiled and nodded. I loaded my three bags into the cart and went on my merry way.

That was a special moment for me. I felt like I was able to bless someone who clearly needed the money more than I did. Then, God specifically answered my request. He was walking right beside me. He always is, of course. But it's another thing when you can really feel and sense it in a special way.

Then I said, "Okay, God, let's go on our walk now. Want to show me more things?" Now this story may sound a bit weird, but what happened next meant a lot to me. I went to a neighborhood I'd been to few times, up a steep hill. I looked to see if God wanted to reveal Himself or show me anything.

I stumbled on a house in the midst of demolition. One side of the house was open so you could see what all the old rooms looked like.

Something very curious caught my eye: the wallpapering inside one of the rooms. It was in the same pattern I'd had as a child. I even had a chance to grab a portion off the wall and take it with me for a scrapbook to remember this date with God.

The House Under Demolition, Yellow Flowered Wallpaper

Heather (sister) and Cheryl in her old room, same wallpaper

Now, to understand why this meant something to me, I should explain the context. The day God led me to this house was during a season of my life God was healing me of some events that happened in the past. Traumatic memories existed from that childhood home. Yet, God was demolishing strongholds from back then, and healing me of past abuse. He'd even sent me a dream before this walk about that house that matched part of what I was looking at.

I really felt like God was right by my side that day saying, "See? I wanted to show you this. That time of your life is being demolished. Torn down and put away." He used the visual of this house I was standing in front of to remind me of that. (And His healing work was thorough!)

That little piece of wallpaper I'd saved that day in November 2004 got thrown out in 2005 when toxic mold ate my apartment.

As God was shedding my past out of my life, all of my old possessions went with it. Including old journals that had chronicled years of difficult pain. The only thing that got saved was what God led me to type into my computer in advance to write *Finally Fearless* and *Finally the Bride*. I had no idea when I felt led to type specific journal entries that I was going to lose everything I hadn't recorded into my computer.

So in the story I just told you, God answered my request to see a specific person to bless with those recyclables. I loved turning over about 50 cans when they worked so hard to find just one out of someone's trash. Then to end up on a walk where God showed me a slice of the healing work He was doing in me from my childhood—where we were in progress—was meaningful.

That was just one date with God. One Prayer Walk.

Later, God led me to take the same walk, telling me the house was gone and all cleared up. And indeed, it was true. The lot was empty upon my return.

These examples show how if we just take that time with God and get together with Him alone, He can show up. He can speak. He can bless. He can heal. He can even make us laugh. I have so many memories of laughing on these Prayer Walks.

Another time when I was single, I was crying out to God about my missing love story. I used story terms like Act One, Act Two, Act Three. Climax of the story. Foreshadowing, which often was wrapped in GodWinks, the little hints He'd give me about my love story to come.

I was praying—in truth, I was complaining—about how I really wanted to be in Act Three of my love story instead of continuously stuck in the many Act Two crises.

Guess what happened? I felt nudged by God to walk to a particular park that day. Upon arrival, I

saw a car parked there that had a license plate that
said, "Third Act."

I laughed. I was encouraged. How's that for a
GodWink? God heard my prayer and gave me
something tangible to see that was more than a
coincidence. Especially when you couple it with the
fact that I felt led to walk to a park I wasn't planning
to go to. I only went because I felt like God wanted
me to.

I'd like to say that the Almighty Love Story
Writer moved me into "Act Three" right away. For
me, that was defined by my real husband showing
up and sweeping me off my feet. It took about
another eight months before I went on that first date
with Chris. Just two months after taking that photo,
God brought Chris and me back into each other's
lives after 10 years of being out of touch. So God was
at work penning Act Three of my love story. I just
didn't recognize it right away.

Ironically, while writing this chapter, I looked
back at that photo of that Third Act license plate. I
noticed the month and date on the plate was
February 2011. Chris and I got engaged on February
18, 2011. The plate gave me its additional wink after
the fact.

Naturally, it helped to have a camera nearby
during these walks so I could preserve these
memories. I never went on a prayer walk without a
camera for this reason. I didn't want to miss saving

something as a souvenir of my dates with God.

No surprise, there was another time I needed encouragement about a promise God had made me. I asked Him if, during our walk, He could show me something with a particular name on it. (You know. If He wasn't too busy or anything.)

Before I finished praying (that never happens), a large truck passed right in front of me with that name emblazoned on it. It was so fast I didn't have time to get my camera out. Regardless, I appreciated the GodWink and encouragement from God that my promise was still in play, even if it was taking Him all the livelong day to bring it to pass.

I wish God were as fast at the delivery of those answers to prayer. At least He was answering my need for encouragement.

During another season, God often used the metaphor of the Potter and the Clay with me. In other words, He's the Potter and I'm the lumpy clay in need of molding, pinching, kneading, shaping, and yes, even firing in that hot kiln, to be useful. I told a friend about this and that I'd really like to see a license plate that had the Bible reference Psalm 40 on it, which talks about miry clay. And low and behold, during our walk that day, God led us to a car that had Psalm 40 as its license plate!

Yes, these things actually do happen. Some may try to pass these moments off as coincidences. They may try to say God had nothing to do with. I don't buy it!

Another time, in a different state and on a different coast, God showed me another car. Same Bible chapter on a different license plate. That time, I didn't ask for it, but I did need some encouragement. I felt like God was there to say, "Hi, I see you." I did get pictures of both plates.

Why not accept God's encouragement when He gives it? I can't say this happens every time I ask for it. Yet, when it does, I celebrate by capturing photos. And I hope you will too.

Side note: I'm purposefully not sharing photos of license plates for privacy reasons of the owners. I suggest you do not post them as well with your blogs or on social media. Do save them for yourself. We can use all the encouragement God offers, right?

I like that God shows up, even when I don't ask Him to. Yet part of the fun of a Prayer Walk with GodWinks is when I ask for something and He shows me. Or He surprises me with something that only He knows what it would mean to me, like that house with my old childhood wallpaper. Or some kind of inside joke between us. He follows up moments like that with words of encouragement or instruction or correction when I need it.

I'll share one last story before I send you on your next Prayer Walk. When I was writing *The Ultimate Gift*, I felt like I was to be like the grandson character, Jason Stevens, and give away some money. His grandfather, Red Stevens, had given him an assignment with a certain amount of money he was supposed to give away.

One day, I felt like my assignment would be to pay a particular person's rent for that month. Naturally, I did what I love to do most: went on a Prayer Walk and asked for God's confirmation.

I saw a car with a plate that said RED DEE. Notice how Red is the character in *The Ultimate Gift* who told Jason to give away money. I felt like this particular license plate was my answer, but I wasn't sure why.

I'm big on asking God for confirmation of His individualized instruction. Naturally, nothing God tells you on these dates should ever contradict Scripture. If you think it does, it is not God.

Giving away money, in and of itself, can be a great and charitable thing. It's easy to line that up with Scripture and its suggestion we be generous to those in need.

Naturally, there is never a shortage of needs among many people we know. We can't help every single person. I wanted specific confirmation that, in this instance, this person was God's choice for me to help. There may be some in your life who need money, but that may not be the way God would choose for you to help them. That's why asking Him first needs to happen.

I knew what Red meant as a symbol regarding

giving away money. But how did this tie to my friend? What did Dee have to do with her? I felt like God whispered, "It's your friend's middle name." I replied, "Really? Cool." I knew if that turned out to be true, I'd have my God-confirmation that this was who He wanted me to give away that money to.

I emailed my friend, asked what her middle name was. She replied:

Dee.

I was blown away. Even though I knew He was speaking, having this extra confirmation was so awesome. I wrote back to her: "God wants me to pay your rent."

This friend had been praying for a solution to her financial situation, and God used me to do it. It was a faith-builder for me and for her. God had also blessed me through writing that film to be able.

Until God allowed me to lose almost everything I owned just a few months later through that toxic mold crisis. Then I needed some help. And boy, did God deliver—and mobilize many of His kids to help me—in spades! Maybe they were on Prayer Walks when God told them to help me, too.

Are you picking up on the fact that dating God is an adventure in faith? It takes unexpected twists and turns, but having God by your side on this walk of faith makes it worth it!

I hope my sample stories are an encouragement to you. Some people would think my stories are a little nutty, or they might try to reason that everything happened purely by coincidence. But I know these were more than coincidences. They were GodWinks. I know God was with me on those walks, saying hello, guiding and encouraging me.

Now I want you to take your turn. This is another one of those dates you'll want to take multiple times. If you start to see God's hand showing up like this on your Prayer Walks, you'll get addicted to it. It's an experience like nothing else, to know the God of the universe walks by your side.

So, go on a Prayer Walk, ask God to wink at you. Give Him freedom to do it His way or ask for specifics or be ready for a mix of both. He can surprise you as well.

Are you praying about something specific? Then pray about it as you go on your date. See if God will supply an answer. Or just let Him love on you and show up with any messages He desires. Both ways can be fun. Both ways can really energize your prayer life and allow you to experience being on real and interactive dates with God.

Date 8
Get Alone in Nature

Location: A place out in nature, like a waterfall, a
    mountain, a beach, flower garden.
Supplies: A camera.
Reading: Read whole chapter before your date.

$\mathcal{I}$ love being out in nature. The woods, the
mountains, the beach, waterfalls, brooks, streams,
anywhere there are flowers, pretty trees or just fresh,
outdoor air.

There's something about being outside that
makes me feel closer to the God who created it all.
Or the One who inspired humans to be so creative in
the way they plant gardens, or even how they design
architecture. Since I believe that God is the most
creative Being in the universe, I appreciate the ways

He's inspired others to be artistic.

It's not surprising that whenever I need to clear my head — or when, historically, I had gone through break ups — the first place I run is the beach.

While we can have quiet times uninterrupted at home, it's just not the same as getting away in nature.

The mountains, the beaches, nature trails, the woods, lakes. The list is endless. Now, you may not live near all of those. But you will benefit if you take time to pinpoint some of these places and put them on your list for dates with God.

We used to live in California where beaches were plentiful. Now that we're in Georgia, the mountains and lakes are closer. Thankfully, some are close enough to escape to. Since God created the earth, nothing makes me feel closer than stepping into nature.

This date is simple. Pinpoint a place you'd like to go. Either your favorite place in nature or a new place you'd like to explore. Bring a camera. If that's your phone, that's okay. Just remember not to let it distract you from your alone time with God.

Practice the Golden Rule: treat God the way you'd like to be treated on a date. I don't know about you, but I like attention to be on me!

Go exploring. Take beautiful pictures of whatever you see. Allow God to lead your walk or your "sit down time" to watch a sunrise or a sunset.

Ask Him to help you capture the beauty. Then later, as a memento of your date, you can print those photos. I have lots of photos from various dates that I save in folders on my computer. Print-worthy ones just might get framed.

There are times I've taken walks with God and asked Him to show me His beauty. He's shown me a double rainbow. A spectacular sunset. (I especially love the ones that look like rays are coming down from heaven.) Fog clearing when it was supposed to be a cloudy day. Sun peeking out of fluffy, cumulus clouds.

I haven't seen Jesus' face in a set of clouds. Maybe a cross or two. But you get the idea. Keep your eyes open and be ready to capture whatever He shows you on camera. Also relax and enjoy the sights. Don't just make it a photography trip. Allow yourself to feel 'still' before Him. Maybe He'll even whisper in your ear. Or maybe He'll just enjoy sitting silently and amicably beside you.

That's all for this simple date. Like others, this is one you can repeat as many times as you'd like. As many places as you'd like to go. The next date takes this whole nature thing a step further.

Date 9
Illustration in Nature

Location: A place out in nature, like a waterfall, a
      mountain, a beach, flower garden.
Supplies: A camera and a journal.
Reading: Read whole chapter before your date.

$\mathcal{E}$ven though I'm asking you to get back out into
nature, this date has a different spin on it. The last
one was just to appreciate the beauty of God's
creation and handiwork. To breathe it in. This one
takes a deeper look at a part of creation to allow God
to speak to you through it.

For this date, I'd like to focus on God's artistic
fingerprints in nature and what He may want to
show you or teach you through it. I'd love for you to
pick a place you find beautiful, outside. Take a

journal. Then ask God to show you an illustration in nature that applies to your life or something you are wrestling with or pondering.

Think flowers, insects, butterflies, plants, trees or whatever captures your attention. Write a journal entry with insights that He shows you through His handiwork. The way it functions, grows, rebirths, the way it demonstrates a special principle that you can apply to a current situation in your life.

One time, a friend of mine said he was watching ants make their anthill. He felt like just watching them gave him spiritual insights about work, planning ahead, diligence, and other lessons God revealed to his heart in the moment.

That's what this date is about: get into nature and allow God to speak to you through it.

An example I'd like to share ties to observing a beautiful flower that was all over our neighborhood in California: morning glories. There were many of them along the driveway of our apartment.

My husband took photos of those flowers for me during two times of day, for the blog that was inspired by them and how they change. (I may be biased, but I think he captured this beautifully with his camera). I'll include those here with the blog itself. This will give you an example of what I have in mind for today's date with God. This entry was written in 2012, after we'd been married a year and still lived in California.

Morning Glory Blog

Psalm 30:5b "Weeping may stay for the night, but rejoicing comes in the morning."

Everyone who knows me almost immediately thinks of the color purple. My purple feathered pen. The name of my production company, Purple PenWorks. My insistence on wearing purple practically every day of my life.

Outside my apartment is a stunning display of morning glory flowers. They're deep purple and blue, and they look like trumpets, ready to herald good news.

When they are open, that is.

They blossom in the morning and especially when it's sunny. They can go into hiding by nightfall or on cloudy days. Sometimes, a few of them refuse to come out, even when the rest of the flowers around them are showing off their colors.

Have you ever had one of those days where you wanted to go into hiding? You didn't want anyone to see your face because they'd be able to read the distress all over it?

There were seasons of my life where I felt like I had nothing to "trumpet," nothing to shout from the rooftops or celebrate. Every day started the same and ended the same, with me closing up into myself—just like those flowers that hide their beauty.

I knew in God's Word it said that while weeping may remain for the night, joy would come in the morning. I often wondered which morning and what calendar God was referring to. I felt more like I was in mourning: mourning the loss of dreams, hopes, time frames, and progress in life. Where I wanted to be by that time in my life. Many mornings came with tears still on the brink. That lump still near my throat. Where was this joy I kept reading about?

This was a long season I call *waiting*.

It was a season of longing.

A season of trying to cling desperately to hope, but finding it in short supply.

When I was in my early twenties, God made me a promise that one day I would get married. I thought that sounded awesome because it had been my desire since I was a young teen. I was happy to hear this was something God had for me.

What God failed to mention was that it would take 16 more years of waiting before His promise would even become a remote possibility. A long wait that would be an adventure in faith.

I would be almost 40 years old when love would finally show up in my life and I could take that long-awaited walk down the aisle. God didn't warn of the trials, the heartbreaks, the journey to come. While I felt ready to blossom much sooner, God would have me in the shade for over a decade and a half of waiting.

Yet still, God wanted me to hold onto hope.

Often, He reminded me of that precious promise from many years ago. Sometimes, the reminders hurt. When I managed to keep my heart in a place of contentment, any reminder of that missing promise-to-come would kick up that desire like wildfire; contentment would be out the window. I would assume if God brought up the topic, the time was imminent. Oh, how many times I would be wrong!

And yet, God still asked for my faith; He still asked for my hope.

It was through the fire of waiting that God refined me, built my trust in Him, prepared me for marriage, taught me to love unconditionally, and showed off His extraordinary sense of impeccable timing.

What God wanted from me was absolute surrender. A surrender of my purple pen. (The pen I would use to write in my journals from a young age about how I thought my love life should go. I made that purple pen a character in *Never the Bride.* I used that purple pen to write *Finally the Bride: Finding Hope While Waiting.* And waiting. And waiting.)

God didn't want me to steal back the pen once I gave it up to Him, during all those times I didn't like what He was writing. He was definitely not taking any of my suggestions—for timelines, for specific guys I'd prayed about, for the changes I ached for.

God surprised me by writing something completely different. Almost seventeen years after God first promised me that one day I'd get married, He reintroduced me to a friend from long ago, Chris Price. I'd met Chris just barely a year or so after God first made me that promise of marriage. We lost touch after a few years of being casual friends, then reconnected over a decade later in 2010.

Chris knew right away there was something to this reconnection. (Wise man that he is, Chris kept that tidbit to himself and waited for God to talk to me about the future of *us*.)

With Chris, instead of me trying to convince God like many times in the past to "give this guy to me," God was trying to convince me to say "yes" to this man. So, what did I do?

I said no.

For six months, I said no.

I had my ideas about what I wanted, and this idea of God's didn't fit my plan. But God wanted me on His plan. Slowly, He worked on my heart. He revealed to me what His best was.

Once I was willing to walk through the door and give Chris a chance, everything moved rather swiftly. Once I started cooperating with God's plan and stopped fighting it, I stepped into the best, most loving relationship I've ever experienced. (Well, outside of my Heavenly Father, that is.)

For the first time in my life, I fell in love with someone who actually loved me in return. Completely and unconditionally. That had never happened to me before, in almost forty years of life.

I could have continued to say no.

I could have missed God's best.

What's funny, in hindsight, I see so clearly why God chose this amazing man for me. In the beginning, I may not have been able to see it. But now, I see the extraordinary gem I could have lost, had I continued to say "no" to God's perfect plan.

Do you ever get impatient in the waiting seasons? Do you get distressed? I had no idea, during the wait, why God had me "on hold" for so long (also known as "the holy pause" button).

As sappy as it may sound, my husband was worth the wait. He was worth the pain and anguish those years of waiting brought into my life. When I think back on the people I wished God would have given me, I have no doubt now why God said "no" to me every time.

When God says, "It's not time yet," trust that He knows what He's talking about. He knows what He's saving you *from* (and *for*).

Whenever I get impatient for God to move in other areas of life, I try to remember how He had my best interests in mind with the timing of my marriage. He's still trustworthy with the timing of the rest of my life.

If you are in a waiting season—no matter what you are waiting for—try not to give up hope. Hope can only make your heart sick when it's a hope we have given up on. Trust that if what you are waiting for isn't here it's either not for your best or it's not the right time. I can attest that though weeping may remain for a night (or even many nights), joy will come in the morning.

Meanwhile, do not hide or shrink away, like those flowers that refuse to show off their colors. The world needs your beauty, that unique contribution that only you can make.

Even while waiting, you can still shine.

That blog was written years ago. But I still remember afresh what God taught me through those flowers. The illustration was clear. So my hope for your date is for you to allow God to show you something, to illustrate something to you with His creative, artistic hand.

Spend some time alone with the most creative Artist we know. On your date, ask Him to show you something in nature and to give you illustrations or applications for your life. Journal about it. Take photos to go with it.

If it's worth sharing, consider posting it as a blog. Maybe even blow up a photo that you take, if it's something beautiful like a morning glory, to remind you of this special time you spent alone with the Lord. We framed the picture of the open, purple morning glory and put it on our wall at home.

I hope you enjoy this time where God can use

His own creation to speak to you. Just like with other dates, feel free to repeat this one many times.

Just keep your eyes open and be still before Him. Wait and see what He will show you, teach you, and guide you to learn through His creation.

Date 10
Bible Roulette

Location: A quiet place in a park with a picnic table or set up a blanket on the grass.

Supplies: A picnic lunch, a journal, a Bible (a printed copy, non-electronic).

Reading: Read chapter during your date.

Sometimes, the best way to get to know someone is to read their autobiography. You may have had countless chats with a friend or date or family member. But you will always find new nuggets about them that they'd include in writing their stories.

When I wrote my autobiography, *Finally Fearless: Journey from Panic to Peace,* I specifically remember two responses about the book.

From my mother and my husband.

Both of them said: "This doesn't even sound like you. I can't believe you went through all that."

Some of it, they may have heard me share. Other details came out as I processed them with pen and paper while writing most of that book long before I got married. Plus, God had healed me so much that I no longer seemed like the broken person who penned those pages. Yet still, it's part of my history.

For example, that autobiography explains my extreme sensitivity when people don't listen to me. Reading about me may help a person know to avoid doing something that will make me feel unheard.

In a similar way, as we grasp God's personality as revealed in His Word, we may also change our behavior according to His likes, His dislikes, His desires, His heart.

For example, one thing is clear in His Word: God does not like it when people do not believe Him or when we doubt Him. Does knowing this change our behavior as we grow more in love with Him? It should.

The Bible is what you could call God's Story. Reading it is one of the best ways to get to know Him, His personality, and His Story. God inspired many writers to write about Him, His Son Jesus, and the Holy Spirit. So, how about we take the time to get to know who God is, as revealed in the Bible?

Even though this book champions spending time with God, speaking to Him directly, watching for His hand out in nature, I never want to diminish the importance of diving into *His autobiography*, the Bible.

Your Turn

For today's date, enjoy your picnic with God. I hope where you sit is free from distractions, away from other park visitors.

Play the game known as "Bible Roulette." You know the one. You open the Bible to a random verse and read it. Ask what God wants to show you. Reflect, meditate on the verse or passage He leads you to. Journal about it. Repeat this as many times as you want to on this date. Once you feel He's given you all the insight He intends from one verse, "roll" again.

Open, point, read, reflect.

Reading comprehension has never been one of my gifts. I know that's a surprise for a writer. Those standardized tests were terrible for me. Don't ask me what I got on my SAT because I failed by most people's standards. I think my entire score in math and verbal was what most people get on just one part.

I had to depend on my 3.94 grade point average in undergrad to get a partial scholarship to grad school because I performed so poorly on the GRE.

The administration lady asked me if I'd like to retake the GRE — clearly I was smart enough to get a higher grade, right? Not when it comes to those tests. So for me, reading takes a great deal of concentration even though I'm not even remotely A.D.D. I have laser sharp focus for just about every activity, except reading.

It takes much work for me to read and understand what I read, let alone remember. Journaling about what I read helps a lot. Taking notes during sermons keeps me engaged. But I need the Holy Spirit's insights to interpret the Bible. That is what I want you to ask for today as well.

Today's focus is on random passages of the Bible, where you feel led to read.

Occasionally, I will open the Word, point to a verse, and it says something like, "Esau has a hairy back." So, what can God possibly speak to me through silliness like that? (Unless I need help with something physical I'm self-conscious about.)

Let's just say God has a sense of humor. The time I landed on that verse, I had just joked with God: "Lord, I want to point to a verse and ask You to speak to me through it, please. Just don't let it be 'Esau has a hairy back.'"

Sure enough I shut my eyes, opened the Bible and pointed. Guess what verse my finger landed on? Yep! Hairy back, folks. I think God was just playing with me, showing that He knows how to laugh.

So now it's your turn. Start playing. Don't be afraid to laugh if He shows you something that seems nonsensical.

Whatever God shows you, capture it in the journal you began at the start of this *Dates With God* journey.

Date 11
You are Wonderfully Made

Location: A quiet place in a park with a picnic table or set up a blanket on the grass.

Supplies: A picnic lunch, a journal, a Bible. (A different translation than NIV if you have one. Electronic is fine.)

Reading: Read chapter during your date.

This date is similar to the Bible Roulette Date, only this time I'm asking you to focus on one portion of God's Word.

Psalm 139:1-18.

I love this chapter because of how specific it is about how God created us. How much He loves us and made us on purpose. (Hairy back and all!)

I want you to feel His outpouring of love by

spending this date reading this love letter He's written about you. About your creation. About how He crafted you just so, how much He loves and pays attention to you. Take your time with this one, nibbling on it like a savory treat.

I suggest you read the NIV version that I've provided in this chapter, at the beginning of your date. Get familiar with it as a whole. Then go back and read one or two verses at a time. Ask God how this applies to you and how He feels about you. Write it down.

Then reread the chapter in your other Bible translation and see if it offers you additional insights.

By the end of this date, this journal entry should contribute another love letter to you from God.

Just to make sure you know and hear this: God doesn't make mistakes, Sisters. Enjoy your journey through the chapter where God tells you how He knows you and how you are wonderfully made by Him.

Psalm 139:1-18
You have searched me, LORD, and You know me. 2 You know when I sit and when I rise; You perceive my thoughts from afar. 3 You discern my going out and my lying down; You are familiar with all my ways. 4 Before a word is on my tongue You, LORD,

know it completely. 5 You hem me in behind and before, and You lay Your hand upon me. 6 Such knowledge is too wonderful for me, too lofty for me to attain. 7 Where can I go from Your Spirit? Where can I flee from Your presence? 8 If I go up to the heavens, You are there; if I make my bed in the depths, You are there. 9 If I rise on the wings of the dawn, if I settle on the far side of the sea, 10 even there Your hand will guide me, Your right hand will hold me fast. 11 If I say, "Surely the darkness will hide me and the light become night around me," 12 even the darkness will not be dark to You; the night will shine like the day, for darkness is as light to You. 13 For You created my inmost being; You knit me together in my mother's womb. 14 I praise You because I am fearfully and wonderfully made; Your works are wonderful, I know that full well. 15 My frame was not hidden from You when I was made in the secret place, when I was woven together in the depths of the earth. 16 Your eyes saw my unformed body; all the days ordained for me were written in Your book before one of them came to be. 17 How precious to me are Your thoughts, God! How vast is the sum of them! 18 Were I to count them, they would outnumber the grains of sand — when I awake, I am still with You.

I hope today you are encouraged as you feel God's love shower over you on this date. My prayer is that He shows you divine insights into who you are to Him.

Date 12
Dance With God

Location: A quiet, roomy place at home (unless you're brave and want to dance in public).
Supplies: Praise and worship music.
Reading: Read whole chapter before your date.

*E*ven if you're not single, you probably remember what it was like to be in that space of wondering, "Who am I going to marry?" "Is it him?" "How about that guy over there?"

A common time of angst for me was around birthdays. Did you fret around that time as well? (Or are you fretting now because you're still in that waiting season?) If so, I feel for you. I know what it's like.

If you're single, have you been praying,

declaring, laminating the idea that, "This will be the year, Lord"? Yeah, I did that too. I had many birthdays pass by with me still being alone.

The story of *Never the Bride* was born out of this angst. I often complained to God about this. It included my angst over going to parties and social events alone.

A beloved friend — who honestly was not trying to aggravate me — said I should go to these parties as if the Holy Spirit were my date. By my side.

But you know what? When you show up at a party and the guy you fanned a flame for shows up with his arm around another young lady, walking in with the Holy Spirit doesn't always *feel like* enough. Let's just be honest.

Yet, this long (and drawn out) season birthed something in me. The lonelier I got, the more I pressed into God.

The more time I spent with God — on dates — the more I wanted to spend time with Him. The hungrier I got for those moments alone. Especially because when He did show up in special, tangible ways — the ways I hope He's been showing up on your dates so far — it can get addictive.

I don't mean to imply that if you don't sense something tangible, He's not there. He absolutely is. But the more He shows up in ways you can point to as a special kiss from heaven, the more you want Him to. The more experiences you crave. The hungrier you get for that closeness.

This book series was born out of the inspiration from that season of my life when I was single, waiting, angsty, frustrated, annoyed. You name it, I felt it.

In *Never the Bride*, Jessie runs a business called Stone Serenades, which helps men pop the question to their women, to propose in elaborate and creative ways. Jessie's ex-boyfriend shows up to hire her to stage his proposal to the woman he left Jessie for...you know the one. The blonde that made her so self-conscious about her brunette locks. Jessie's ex is just the clientele she was looking for, right?

In this scene, she's in the midst of a conversation with God when her ex suddenly walks around the corner. When she falters a bit at her ex's announcement that he's engaged—when he flat out refused to marry Jessie—God stands right behind her, protectively. She even feels Him stand against her shoulder blade, keeping her steady.

That is the God I know.

I may have fictionalized these types of moments for the sake of humor (and sometimes drama). But He is the God who stands behind us, beside us, or walks in front of us, depending on what we need.

Another special scene in *Never the Bride* was mentioned in *Dating God 101*, the moment from the script that inspired this whole book series.

Jessie's dance with God.

Allow me to set the scene for you:

Jessie surrendered her purple pen to God to write her love story. However, He's been slow to move that pen. So she thinks. She can't see evidence He's at work. (She forgets He works most often behind-the-scenes.)

Jessie gets sidetracked by men that God is not writing into her story. Her birthday is getting closer. She asks God to take care of this problem of her singleness on time. God has no intention of doing so.

God wants Jessie to Himself.

By this point in the story, she jokes with God about it. I'd like to share a slice of the dialogue exchange from the script. Please read this with the snarky sense of humor it's meant to have:

> GOD: Would you do me the honor of spending your birthday with me?
>
> JESSIE: Are you...you're not asking me on a date, are you?
>
> GOD: (smiles) That would be highly inappropriate.
>
> JESSIE: Is this your way of telling me my husband isn't gonna show up by then?
>
> GOD: So, are you available?
>
> JESSIE: Right. I'll sit at a table talking to you. My spectators will think I'm schizo. And I'll have to pay.

GOD: Well?
JESSIE: Okay.
GOD: Okay?
JESSIE: Yes.
GOD: You'll go?
JESSIE: Yes.

Despite what the dialogue says, God is, indeed, asking Jessie out on a date. He allows her to find $60 in cash someone dropped, to pay for the meal out. (That's fiction for ya!) She asks for a table for two, talks to Him across from the table. Yes, her spectators think she's nuts. They think she's talking to herself. By this point in the story, she doesn't care.

Jessie enjoys the company of God Almighty much more than she cares about what other people think.

God encourages the restaurant's pianist—through the whisper of suggestion that only God can pull off—to play Jessie's favorite love song. (Have you experienced those moments when something happens in public that you sense God orchestrated just to say "Hello" to you?)

Then God invites her into a dance.

Jessie's afraid she'll look silly at this swanky restaurant, dancing alone from everyone else's point of view. Remember: No one else can see God. But then, she decides to do it. She goes onto the dance floor, uncaring about appearances and the opinions of others, and enjoys a beautiful dance with God. In other words, she goes into a public place alongside the Holy Spirit and ends up having the time of her life.

This is what today's date is about.

I'm not suggesting you go to a swanky restaurant and start using their dance floor alone, unless you want to.

This is the kind of date that could benefit from privacy and a roomy space. This can be in your home when no one else is around, your bedroom. Wherever you choose. Make sure you have room to move.

Put on your favorite praise and worship tunes or music station and just dance.

Dance with God.

Express your love for Him through moving to praise music. It can be freeing. Just like Jessie lets herself go and dances with God, I want you to get lost in your dance with God, too.

Now, some denominations don't care for dancing. However, I see this date as one inspired by David, who danced before the Lord with wild abandon. Second Samuel 6:14 says, "Wearing a linen ephod, David was dancing before the LORD with all his might."

In 1 Chronicles 15:29, it shares how Saul's daughter saw David dancing from a window. I like how it says he was, "Dancing and celebrating."

This is meant to be playful, Ladies. Dance with God. Dance for Him with all your heart. Play and have fun. Even laugh a little (or a lot).

Dance your way right into God's heart and allow Him to dance His way into yours.

Date 13
Psalm 151

Location: A quiet place, preferably outside, like a park
bench or near a water fountain or flower garden.
Supplies: A journal.
Reading: Read chapter during your date.

I know what you're thinking. *There is no Psalm 151.
I just checked my Bible. It ends at Psalm 150, see?*

So, how about you write it?

A few dates ago, you dove into God's Word,
including one of his love letters about you (Psalm
139). How about next, you write a letter to Him, in a
similar writing style as the writers of the psalms?
Call it Psalm 151 or whatever you would like.
However, unlike Date 4's love letter called, "How
Do I Love Thee," in this one, you are free to integrate

requests with your praises.

David often went back and forth between prayers and praises in his psalms. Sometimes it's neat to study his transitions from distress to encouragement. Praying *affected* his heart.

For this date, you can do the same. You can even let God know if you're distressed or hurting. Not that He doesn't already know, but sometimes it's therapeutic to get that out in writing.

My suggestion for your version of Psalm 151 is to write it out like a work of poetry. Write from the heart. Maybe even start some verses with "I praise You because..." or "I worship Your name because..." and fill in the blanks.

Then go into any concerns that are on your heart that you would like God to address. Just try to finish your psalm on a positive note, or a word of praise. Also, note how often David ends his psalms with statements of faith and confidence in God. He allowed prayer to uplift his downcast heart, then invited God to help and lead him.

There are many examples throughout Psalms where men of God cried out in pain and fear.

For example, consider Psalm 10:1 that reads, "Why, LORD, do You stand far off? Why do You hide yourself in times of trouble?" Isn't it comforting to read the prayers of others who also felt alone, felt despair, and cried out to God through journaling? They wrote out their feelings, honestly, even though

God had never left them.

Here is a wonderful example King David wrote during a time of despair.

> Psalm 13:1-6
> "How long, LORD? Will You forget me forever? How long will You hide Your face from me? How long must I wrestle with my thoughts and day after day have sorrow in my heart? How long will my enemy triumph over me? Look on me and answer, LORD my God. Give light to my eyes, or I will sleep in death, and my enemy will say, 'I have overcome him,' and my foes will rejoice when I fall. But I trust in Your unfailing love; my heart rejoices in Your salvation. I will sing the LORD's praise, for He has been good to me."

Notice David's attitude shift by the end, going back to faith in God, going back to praising God despite his pain. When you write out your prayers, if you hear a response from God, write out His answer back to you as well. Write down any comforting verses He leads you to.

Be honest, be open, share praises and concerns. Be ready for God to listen to your heart.

Date 14
Building Faith Through Milestones With God

Location: A quiet place at home.

Supplies: A Bible, your journal, plus any old journals you've kept.

Reading: Read chapter during your date.

$\mathcal{E}$very date with God should build intimacy, friendship, romance, and faith. For this particular volume of *25 Dates With God*, I wanted to integrate specific dates to build your faith, like this one.

There is no question that life has ups and downs, highs and lows, joys and sorrows. When you think back on your life, do you have those moments where you have fond memories that carry you through more difficult seasons?

Anyone who's ever battled depression may have heard their friends or family try to encourage them with such sentiments as, "Don't worry, life will get better." Or "This too shall pass" or "Better times are ahead." We've all heard it; we've all been in seasons where those words were hard to believe.

Sometimes, it's the memory of better times in the past that can carry us through a difficult season. They supply much needed hope. This date is about Building Milestones With God, to take you through an exercise where you can chart milestones — significant memories — you share with God.

What does that mean?

Psalm 77 was written by Asaph during a time of distress. He cried out to God, questioned Him, and then used reminders of specific past miracles and blessings to build his faith while waiting for God to answer to his current pain. There wasn't an answer from God in the moment as Asaph wrote. Yet Asaph did a wise thing to remind himself that God does show up in times of need. (God may not always be predictable as to *when* He'll answer, but He does.)

Begin this date opening your Bible to read Psalm 77. Look at Asaph's cries to God and then his list of moments where he takes inventory of what God did for him historically.

Done reading now? Good. (Don't skip that part.) This psalm is the basis for me creating the *Milestones With God* assignment for you to do in this chapter.

Before moving forward, I'd love for you to take time to read 2 Samuel 22. This is one of my favorite chapters about God showing up to help one of His kids, David.

I love how the chapter goes into how David cried out to God. God heard him. He burned in anger about David's situation (v. 8), and then He came down (v. 10). God didn't just stay far away from David and watch. He literally came down to help. God scattered David's enemies (v. 15). Then He even reached down to grab David out of those "deep waters" (v. 17) and rescued him. God rescued him because He delights in His kids (v. 20).

When we need God, He is ready to help us. He will intervene. We can't always predict how He'll show up. By our definition, it may feel like God is late in doing so or not taking our desired actions. But He always answers.

Though many don't think of God as having an interactive relationship with us in our lives, the Bible is full of examples of personal, divine encounters.

Here are some of my favorite stories in the Bible where God showed up, building milestones with some of His other kids. Feel free to read any of these when you are in need of encouragement about God's involvement in our lives.

God's Interventions:

Parting the sea for the Egyptians (Exodus 14).

Gideon overhearing the dream and being encouraged for battle (Judges 7:9-15).

Elijah being fed by ravens. God uses the widow, supplies food. Elijah asks God to heal her son. (1 Kings 17) Then in 1 Kings 19 after his mountaintop type of experience, he was depressed. God showed up there, too, to talk to him and help him rest.

King Solomon asks for wisdom, in a dream, and God gives it to him to help with a court case (1 Kings 3).

God helped the fellow inmate (cupbearer) remember Joseph the dream interpreter from prison, 2 years later (Genesis 41).

Releasing the chains of the prisoner Peter (Acts 12).

Road to Damascus (Acts 9).

Woman at the Well – Jesus' words of knowledge and wisdom being so important to help her (John 4).

My Milestones

Before I get you started on your own Milestones, I want to share how these have been used in my life.

There are times when God *seems* more present than others. When it feels like you are in a dry or quiet season from His voice, it helps to look back. Remember what He's said or done historically to build faith while waiting in the midst of whatever life crisis or challenge is going on.

I did my first Milestones assignment during that season I've mentioned a few times. That "angsty single" season. My "crisis" was feeling like God was taking forever to write my love story. I had a promise to hold onto, that one day I would get married.

You remember that 7-year waiting period of "no dating" from 2003 until my first date with Chris? In those seven years, I had many crises of faith. I often questioned God. Was He really going to show up? Did He really make that promise? Was it just wishful thinking? Was I crazy to believe it?

So I made myself go through this exercise like the psalmist. I wrote out a list of Milestone Moments when I knew for sure God had shown up for me.

I started with ten and thought of so many others that I filled in more than my worksheet could take. I wrote down the incidents, the approximate dates.

Here are some examples:

1. When I lost everything I owned to toxic mold, God told me to watch and see how He'd restore my life. Then I saw gift after gift flow in to help me through that crisis. I was more than restored. God showed off His faithfulness in dynamic ways throughout the seemingly devastating experience.

2. The time when I was a little kid that I believe God inspired two 5-year-old friends to stop a sexual abuser from harassing me anymore. (I share the full story in *Finally Fearless*.)

3. The time God miraculously healed me of mono on Christmas Eve, in answer to my mother's prayers. I was skiing on slopes days later. (Against doctor's orders. They don't always understand divine healings.)

4. The time God allowed me to get kicked out of a BFA acting program in favor of switching over to writing. It hurt at the time, but now I wouldn't trade what I do for anything.

5. The season when God was encouraging me to move to Los Angeles. I moved there on a leap of faith with no job, no place to live. Unlike the planner in me. Yet I knew it was what I was called to do. Within days of arriving, I was in pitch meetings at TV network studios with a director and producer. Just as I was about to fill out apartment applications where they wanted my employment information, a kid's show I had been pitching got its green light and became my work reference. Then, I found a place to live and a roommate. Within a couple of weeks of moving in, I got hired to be a post-production assistant at PAX TV, which was a two-block walk from my new apartment. (Yes, the apartment came first!) I felt like God paved the way so wonderfully after I was willing to take that step of faith and move there.

6. The job to write *The Ultimate Gift* came through after God had promised (prophetically) to open a new door in my profession for me. This was a faith-builder that God delivers on His promises, even if I am still waiting on others.

7. The time God warned me the relationship I thought was heading toward marriage would end. He did so through a series of eight prophetic dreams. It was a painful message, but He loved me enough to warn me in advance. That showed me God cares, especially in the painful moments, to show up, help, and take care of my heart.

Those are just seven examples I wrote down back in 2007. I'm sure you noticed they weren't just happy memories. Yet, they were significant moments where I felt like God helped me.

God was faithful, restorative, protective, or supplied some much-needed direction. Overachiever that I am, I wrote down 27 Milestones Moments the first time I did the assignment.

Even as I typed out this list for you, I felt a stirring in my spirit that God is with me. God hasn't forgotten me. My husband and I have had our own struggles in waiting on God for other promises. Just the act of typing this old list from pre-marriage has been a faith-builder for our present life.

When I did my milestone sheet in 2007, I had many promises about my future husband from the Lord, but none of the payoffs yet. So those didn't make my milestones list back then. They didn't become milestones until God's promises about Chris paid off in reality. All of those formed new milestones.

When Chris and I co-wrote the end of *Finally the Bride*, we shared how God spoke to both of us in advance, for over a decade, about who we'd marry. The type of person He'd chosen for us. We share every one of those setups and payoffs. How intricate God was with details in advance. I won't get into all of those here since it's available in the other book. But that story alone is another long set of milestones with God.

A recent milestone moment for me was when I woke up at 3 a.m. and felt an urgency to pray for my husband's safety on his drives to and from work. (In the ridiculous Atlanta traffic. Seriously. It's worse than Los Angeles.)

Normally, this type of prayer would get my adrenaline pumping and make me nervous and keep me awake the rest of the night. Instead, I gently laid my hand on him, didn't wake him up, prayed over him and his body, and asked his angels to take care of him.

One tradition every morning is my husband texts me when he arrives at work. When I woke up, I checked my phone. He usually gets there by 6:30 a.m. It was 7 a.m., but I didn't have a text. My go-to temptation would have been to freak out. Especially given the prayer time in the middle of the night.

Instead, I reminded myself to trust God with

Chris. Five minutes later, my phone rang. Chris called to tell me he'd been rear-ended on the way to work. He could see it coming; the guy behind him was struggling to stop. Chris' car was between the big truck in front of him and the other truck that skidded and screeched as it tried to stop behind him.

Here's the good news. Even though the guy ran into him, neither of them got hurt. There was no real damage to his car. I immediately felt like God had led me to pray and call forth Chris' protective angels hours earlier on purpose. It was a milestone moment for me, to remind me of God's faithfulness and that prayer works.

The reason we should track our milestones and write them out is to have this journal entry to look back on and remind ourselves of God's prior faithfulness through life's adventures.

Milestones with God Worksheet:
Now it's your turn. I'm suggesting you have this date at home in case you've kept a supply of old journals with notes from past prayers and answers from God. You can use these as a reference when writing up your milestones.

Pinpointing your milestones is best done during a less difficult season of life when you are feeling more positive about where you are and where you've come from. Yet even if you happen to be in a difficult season when you make your list, it's worth doing.

Now it's your turn:

For the time you spend on this date, prayerfully come up with at least 10 moments in your life when God showed up and did something for you. (Examples: salvation, miracles, healings, answered prayers, a time He spoke to you clearly, gave you direction, comforted you.)

Write a brief description of what happened and the approximate date. Refer to this journal entry any time you are faltering in your faith and wondering where God is or what He's doing with your life.

Now that you've written your list, how do you feel? Was it hard to come up with moments or did you have too many to stick with just ten?

Keep in mind that new believers may not have quite as many to write down as those who've shared a long relationship with Jesus as their Savior. And that's okay.

Just remember you can also think back to moments before you believed and see if there were times Jesus was clearly wooing you to Himself. Summoning you to put your trust and faith in Him. The most trustworthy One.

I do think sometimes we forget to give credit to

God for things He has done for us. So if you are having trouble, try to think through times when your life had a blessing or a near-miss disaster and see where you believe God was during that blessing or crisis.

When you feel abandoned by God or struggle in your wait for a prayer to be answered or a promise to be fulfilled, you can remind yourself of the good things God has done in the past. Then you can trust Him during your wait.

I hope this exercise is as much of a faith builder for you as it has been for me. It's one I've repeated over the years — or added to — as God has continued to show Himself strong in my life. I hope you will too.

I just know that some of these dates with God will turn into milestones of their own.

Date 15
Faith in the War Room

Location: A quiet place at home.
Supplies: A bulletin board, colored index cards,
   thumbtacks.
Reading: Read whole chapter before your date.

$\mathscr{I}$'m sure you've heard of the popular movie, *War Room*, the 2015 release of the Kendrick Brothers, makers of *Facing the Giants*, *Fireproof*, and *Courageous*. *War Room* started a revolution among Christians to concentrate on intercessory prayer. For their family, friends, colleagues, even strangers. It was a demonstration of how prayer works.

   I've always been a huge fan of prayer. I like to walk around while I pray, whether I'm at home or outside. Number one, to stay awake. (What is it about prayer that can sometimes lull us to sleep?) And two, to keep me active, engaged, and at war.

When I want to engage in "warring" prayer for myself or others without really being heard, I stay home. It's a little hard to pull off that kind of prayer if you're concerned others will hear you while you're out on a walk.

Karen Abercrombie is a friend of mine and played the delightfully feisty, prayer warrior Miss Clara in *War Room*. I knew I didn't have a closet I could designate for praying like Miss Clara did. Being a writer, I did come up with a creative, space-saving method for my own version of a war room. And it's portable.

I have bulletin boards and colored index cards that I occasionally use when outlining screenplays. I took one of those boards and made it my "War Room Board."

Here's a photo:

I labeled various sections: Family, Friends, Spouse, Career, Church, Neighborhood, World Events, Country, Misc. Then I wrote out prayers for various people, places, groups. This board quickly filled up. (For illustration purposes, I took the photo before I wrote out prayer requests, just for the sake of privacy of those I've been interceding for.) It didn't take long for there to be layers of cards under the various categories.

When time permits, I take out that board and pray for the needs represented. Sometimes I pray for all of them. Sometimes I focus on a specific section or type of prayer.

I also got a plastic index card box to use for answered prayers. When the prayer on a card is answered, it gets removed from the board. I write a note on the back of the card with the answer, the date it was answered, and put it in the box. If a new need comes up due to an answered prayer, I make a new card.

For example, the first answered prayer of my War Room Board was the pregnancy of a friend who'd had multiple miscarriages. When she got pregnant after 5 years of trying again, I immediately wrote out the praise to God that she was pregnant. Then I made a new card to pray for a healthy pregnancy.

So, like me, you may not have a room you can designate for a war room. Do you have access to a bulletin board and colored index cards? You can color code by types of prayer requests or just use color for fun.

Today's date with God is to set up your own *War Room* board. Buy materials if needed. Ask God which needs should be represented. Have your first prayer session to pray over those needs either right after making the board or within a few days after, if time is tight.

While you should include significant prayer requests for yourself and your family so you can have a record of answered prayers later, use this as a tool to intercede for others as well. Give God a chance to highlight people you can pray for.

This is a time I'll suggest you go on social media during a date. A quick look at your newsfeed, like on Facebook, is likely to yield prayer requests of your friends.

Trust me. Your faith will build through this exercise. The more cards you get to remove from that board as answered, the stronger your personal faith will grow. You'll celebrate the victories of friends and family as you see God moving in their lives. You'll have a box of answered prayers to read over, to build your faith.

So what are you waiting for? Time to go to war. The good kind.

Date 16
Your Inner Artist Date

Location: A café, private table in or outside.

Supplies: An Adult Coloring Book on a Christian theme (Psalms or inspirational), colored pencils (or your preferred coloring supplies).

Reading: Read whole chapter before your date.

For this date, find a sidewalk café or coffee shop. I like to be outside, at tables where it may not be quite as loud or distracting as inside. Maybe a non-chain coffee shop that isn't as heavily trafficked.

Let's just get a confession out of the way: I cannot draw. No artistic ability whatsoever. My sister, on the other hand, does beautiful animal artwork. Or she did, until my wonderful nephews showed up and distracted her from her talents to homeschool them. She would take colored pencils and make the most realistic looking animals.

That is not my talent. I can't even draw stick figures. In filmmaking, I often wished I could draw storyboards to express what I wanted out of a shot to my director of photography. However, my people looked like giant potatoes.

So, the moral of this story about my lack of artistic talent is this: To share this date with God, you do not need an ounce of artistic ability or interest.

The number one supply I'd suggest you get for this date is the recently popular adult coloring books. I have several I got for under $10 at discount stores that are Christian, Inspirational, or Psalm themed books. Someone else already did the swirly lines, the parts you color in.

I bought colored pencils, though you can use whatever coloring utensils you prefer. Use crayons for all I care, though they may be a bit fat for the lines. But you know what? Here's an assignment where you may color outside the lines if you so desire. This isn't being graded.

Even if you can draw freestyle, for this particular date, I'd love to suggest you participate with one of those books so you can just relax and color. For another date, in another installment of this book series, we will get the chance to let God inspire us to draw something original.

So, grab coffee or a cappuccino with caramel and whipped cream, a sandwich or salad, and sit at a café table. Then, get artistic.

The point is get alone, get comfortable, and be ready to express yourself.

They call this activity with adult coloring books a stress reliever for a reason. It's calming, gives your mind a break. Also, if you choose a Christian or inspirational themed one, they have lovely sayings and themes you can spend an hour or so absorbing while you color. It is relaxing.

My favorite coloring books feature encouraging Psalms. I can't show examples of those I've colored, since the material is copyrighted. But even these make me look good. All I had to do was follow the lines. I've never been one to color outside the lines. I like law and order, neatness, and items going where they belong. The cool thing is if you and someone else chose the same page, neither would look the same. They show beautiful examples of the same picture and how different they can look by different artists.

So enjoy the amicable silence with God as you concentrate on expressing yourself artistically. Perhaps you'll get to know the creative, artistic aspects of God who chose many colors for His creation.

If you feel God speaks to you about the verse or image on the page, write it down. Maybe even somewhere on the page itself.

And relax! Enjoy the quiet time away with God, away from the distractions of every day life.

Don't be afraid to let your inner artist out, even if, like me, you have no natural talent in this area. This is about you, God, and expressing your creativity.

For this chapter, I'd like to leave you with a verse, Philippians 4:8:

> "Finally, brothers and sisters, whatever is true, whatever is noble, whatever is right, whatever is pure, whatever is lovely, whatever is admirable—if anything is excellent or praiseworthy—think about such things."

This is your day to think on these things, through art.

Date 17
Make Requests Known

Location: A private place where you can pray out loud.

Supplies: A journal.

Reading: Read whole chapter during your date.

$\mathcal{L}$ots of these dates have focused on you praising God and enjoying His company for who He is, not what He can do. I'm sure you've often heard the phrase, "Seek His face, not His hand." I'm encouraging that by keeping the focus of the dates away from our personal needs most of the time and on getting to know God on a deeper level.

But let's just admit it. Sometimes, we want or need something from God. Sometimes, we just want to have a powwow about it with Him, while we go off to be alone with Him. This happens in a dating or marital relationship as well. So, why not with God?

Today's date can happen at any place you choose. On a walk, in your closet, out in nature. I enjoy mixing this up. Sometimes, I want to be home where no one else is so I can talk loudly, freely. I can even cry, without anyone else hearing what is on my heart. Especially if the needs are really private.

I'd like you to be able to talk out loud for this one. Not just journal. Keep it between you and God.

I have also loved taking prayer walks to get me out of the way of distraction during these types of prayers. Also, to give Him the chance to speak or show me something specific related to what I was praying (like during the Prayer Walks with GodWinks style of date).

So feel free during this date to move around if you'd like. You know the setting that would work best for this date.

Let's look at a few verses about bringing our requests to God. He welcomes this.

Philippians 4:6 says, "Do not be anxious about anything, but in every situation, by prayer and petition, with thanksgiving, present your requests to God."

Notice the instructions for presenting your requests to God:

- Fear not
- Pray and petition
- Give thanks

Simple, right?

The word *petition* implies this doesn't have to be a one-sentence prayer or even a one-time prayer. We can go to God more than once with the same need, or for further insights if we need it. Or — let's be real here — when we feel like maybe God didn't hear us the first time. (Of course, He did! But sometimes it just feels good to repeat ourselves, doesn't it? I'm so thankful God is patient with me.)

Just remember to thank God for all He is doing while you wait for what hasn't happened yet. That dream in your heart that hasn't come true. Desire for provision, a new job, a new profession, a new education, a spouse, a child.

Anything.

God can take it and will listen.

He doesn't always answer "yes" and He almost never answers right away. But this also helps foster relationship.

At times, I realized my quest for finding a husband and trusting God with that task brought me closer to God than any other trial. Not only because it lasted so long, but because no one else could fix this for me but Him.

My next favorite passage to ponder when I

want to go to the Lord with requests is Matthew 7:7-12, the section known as "Ask, seek, knock":

> Matthew 7:7-12
> "Ask and it will be given to you; seek and you will find; knock and the door will be opened to you. 8 For everyone who asks receives; the one who seeks finds; and to the one who knocks, the door will be opened. 9 Which of you, if your son asks for bread, will give him a stone? 10 Or if he asks for a fish, will give him a snake? 11 If you, then, though you are evil, know how to give good gifts to your children, how much more will your Father in heaven give good gifts to those who ask Him! 12 So in everything, do to others what you would have them do to you, for this sums up the Law and the Prophets."

I think all of us have lived life long enough to know and understand this doesn't mean God is going to grant our every wish like He's a genie.

However, I do find it comforting to know His heart is to "give good gifts" to His children. I prayed and prayed (and incessantly prayed) about my "Missing Husband." I was tempted to make a *Wanted* poster. I can testify that God did, indeed, give me a good gift. A great gift, actually. But God's idea of a great gift meant giving my husband to me over 17 years after He first promised me I'd one day get married. That hardly falls in line with my definition of great. But it was God's best and that's what matters.

Finally, before you pray, ask God to hear you. Psalm 4:1 says, "Answer me when I call to You, my righteous God. Give me relief from my distress; have mercy on me and hear my prayer."

For this date, I want to give you a chance to express to God what is on your heart.

Evaluate your life right now in these areas:

- Personally
- Professionally
- Spiritually

Is there anything you need God's help with? Is there a tangible need you'd like to ask Him for? Do you need a healing, physically or emotionally? Is there a "promise" you feel God's made you that you'd like to ask Him about that hasn't come to fruition? Do you need clarity or direction? Is He waiting on you or are you waiting on Him? Those sorts of questions.

May God have mercy on you, lead your prayers to Him, and show up in a tangible way on this date that you use to make your requests known before Him. He is capable of doing much more than we could ever ask or think (Ephesians 3:20).

So go ahead and close that closet door or go on that walk, and express your heart to God.

Date 18
Acts of Faith

Location: A quiet place at home.
Supplies: A journal, a Bible.
Reading: Read chapter during your date.

*A*re you going through something in life that could benefit from doing something symbolic? An act of faith?

As mentioned, God has at times given me specific promises. Most often, I've had to wait many years to see them come to fruition. For some promises, I'm still waiting. (In addition to letting me know I have the "gift of faith," I think God is under the impression I also have "the gift of wait.")

My husband did an interesting "Act of Faith" when we were just dating. It was the ultimate symbol of leaving room for God to move. He took his whole family to the photography studio where he worked, asked them to pose for family photos. He asked them all to wear white shirts and blue jeans.

I was clear across the country, so I couldn't come for this family photo session. Besides that, we weren't engaged yet, so I wasn't a part of this family, officially.

And yet, Chris chose to take that photo with one space left empty beside him:

For me.

Without me being there, the photo itself looks a little funny and unbalanced. Yet he had such faith that one day I would be in this family that he left room in the picture for me. It was an amazing symbol of him believing God, that God would work out our relationship and that one day, he could Photoshop me into that picture.

After we got engaged and I was about to fly home a month before the wedding preparations, Chris asked me to pack a white shirt and blue jeans. I had no idea why.

Once in Charlotte, he took me to the studio and told me to wear that outfit.

He took photos of me alone, directing me on how to stand, but wouldn't tell me what they were for. About eight months later, for our first Christmas after we were married, he gave me a gift:

Our family photo.

All of us, in white. It took me a few seconds to notice I was in that photo, but what a surprise. Check out the before and after photo:

Before

After

My point in telling this story is that Chris did this—in faith—that I would be in his family one day. He left room for me. He left room for God to move and put me in his family. This, by definition, is an act of faith.

Since the theme of this particular volume is *Adventures in Faith*, I wanted to give you a chance to think about what your act of faith could be.

What you choose to do for this date may come from a request or two that you prayed about during the last date or it may be something completely different. It could tie to what you are currently contending for, for God to take care of for you.

Has God promised you something that hasn't come to fruition yet? Is there something you can do to show God you believe Him?

Some who feel God has promised them children may move into a home that could accommodate a nursery, even before they are pregnant or going through the adoption process. They do this in faith to show God they are making room for Him to give them a child.

One of my prayer warriors has insisted from the moment she heard about my screenplay, *Never the Bride*, that it would be a movie one day. After I released *Finally the Bride*, she declared that *Never the Bride* wouldn't be *Never the Movie*. It would be *Finally the Movie*. (I liked that expression of faith.)

After she'd had a copy of the screenplay tucked

in a drawer for years, she moved it to the top of her desk where it could get sun every day. Sun is symbolic of bringing life to growing things, right? That was her act of faith on my behalf.

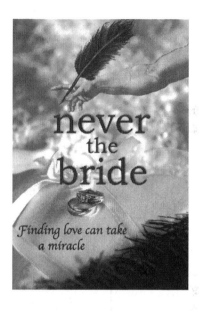

I even made a graphic one time of a green light (since that's symbolic of what happens when a movie gets green lit for production) and printed it next to the book cover and movie poster graphic. I hung this on my desk as an act of faith.

Some acts of faith in my life right now are still contending for answers that are in "wait mode." I haven't seen the fruition. That doesn't stop me from doing acts that show God I have faith in Him to move on my behalf. Especially in areas I cannot control or make happen on my own.

Like getting a movie made.

Some who are sick with terminal illnesses make future plans, acting as though they expect to still be here.

When my dad was in the hospital and needed open-heart surgery, I did an act of faith. I posted a list of goals on his bedpost. Number one on that list was, "Walk Cheryl down the aisle." The nurse asked me when I was getting married. I declared, "I don't know, but he's going to be here for it!"

Dancing with my dad at my wedding in 2011 was one of the most touching parts of the day for me. Having him there was my dream come true that had been taped to his hospital bedpost in 2004.

So, how about you? What are you believing for?

Is there anything you can do on this date to show God you believe Him? You know He can move on your behalf. Can you express to Him that you believe it?

I can't pretend to know what you may put on this list or what you should do to show you believe Him. Or even what act of faith to take that leaves room for God to move. Only you know what is in your heart. What you need, what you want, and what you feel God may have revealed He would like to do on your behalf.

My suggestion is that you write out a prayer about this need. Find some verses in Scripture that

line up with this need and what Scripture says about
God's provision for it. (For example, while waiting
for a husband, I used "God sets the lonely in
families" (Psalm 68:6a). And, of course "It is not
good for the man to be alone" (Genesis 2:18). God
probably got tired of me quoting that one to Him ad
nauseum. As if He didn't already know it was there.
(But there was a man. Alone. Because I wasn't with
him yet, right?)

A word of caution: If God directs it your act of
faith has weight. One tricky part is not turning this
into a "name and claim it" exercise over something
God may not have for you. This is where hearing His
voice is vital. Ask Him what you should believe for,
then take an action to show your unwavering faith.

We don't always know what God is up to or
which desires or needs He intends to answer—at
least not in the way we may hope or expect. But why
not at least give Him the room to move?

So, this date is about choosing your act of faith
and doing it. In what way can you make room for
God's potential answer?

Maybe leaving room for God to move involves
getting rid of something that needs to be gone. An
addiction, like drugs or alcohol, that is getting in the
way of your progression. A bad relationship or
friendship that is getting in the way of you finding
your one true mate.

I had to cut off a male friendship before my

heart would open to Chris. It was painful, but it was definitely an act of faith to give up the comfortable to explore the unknown. And it sure paid off! God was all over it, once I was willing to open my hand and let go.

Some take their act of faith as making a battle plan to get out of debt. They want to make room for more freedom in their budgets for the cares of the Lord. Let's be honest. Being saddled with lots of debt and having to work multiple jobs to cover it is likely to get in the way of other goals we could focus on. So even making a plan to clear that up—and sticking to it—can be its own act of faith.

What would God ask of you today, to show Him your faith? Is there an act of faith you can do tied to a request you uncovered or prayed for on a prior date?

Do the act of faith if that's possible during the date. Or make a battle plan if it's something that will take time.

Allow Him to direct you.

Date 19
The Giving Date

Location: A safe, public area, where you can interact
  with people.
Supplies: Money, small increments.
Reading: Read whole chapter before your date.

Generosity. Giving. Sharing. For some people, this
comes more naturally than others. It comes more
naturally to my husband than myself. I'm such a
meticulous budgeter. I am the one who manages our
finances. Going outside our normal giving can be a
stretch for me.

I would have to admit—embarrassingly so—
that I fall into the camp where sometimes it takes a
push to remind me to be generous. I don't mean
when it comes to tithing the 10% of our gross income

(first fruits) and giving away what God asks us to of our income. That's easy for me. I've been doing that since my dad taught me to when I was 8 years old.

Dad set up three Campbell Soup cans, strung across my canopy bed. He had me label one *Savings*, one *Spending*, and one *Giving*. I'm so thankful I learned those concepts back then so that it was never a shift to think of it as "my" money. Tithing is a no-brainer; it's not a sacrifice. It's obedience.

I'm talking about the above and beyond, the stretching, the giving of yourself, whether through time or resources for the sake of others. Sometimes, for me, it's a whole lot easier to give away money than it is to give away time. But honestly, we need to be able to do both.

In another edition of the *Dates With God* series, we'll go on a volunteer date to give away our time. This particular date will focus on giving away money.

You know what you can handle — big or small. Or a better idea is to ask God what you can handle. Set an amount, grab some cash in small increments, and then watch to see what God will do for you as you go out and ask Him who to bless.

I know it's tempting. But don't skip to the next chapter to avoid this date. Give this a try. I promise you will be more blessed than the one you choose to give to (or the one God highlights to you).

Sometimes, giving means stepping out of your

comfort zone. I, personally, do not like to talk to strangers. Not even a little bit. Unless it's that person who's walking her dogs in my own neighborhood or something that feels safe.

To share where I got this idea ties back to *The Ultimate Gift*. As mentioned before, James Garner's character, Red Stevens, wanted his grandson, Jason, to give away money. Jason got to choose who to give to.

I read many articles about the impact that film had on others. One article and video was about a group of people who, inspired by the film, gave away money. They put $5 bills in their pockets and took to the streets to hand them out. The video was humorous. Some people were afraid to take five bucks. Probably afraid these guys wanted something from them and weren't just offering this as a gift. But it was neat to also see people blessed. You never know when someone is down to their last $5.

The date I am suggesting here involves going out in public and looking for needs you can meet. Go to a safe area or do this with a buddy, if you have a local *Dates With God* friend, or with your husband or boyfriend.

Near us, there are plenty of cute, safe, revitalized "Main Streets" in small downtown areas. They are well populated with families, adorable shops, and restaurants. I'm not talking about trying this on Skid Row, though some are called to that. Go, walk around, and ask God to highlight someone or someone(s) and give away whatever you feel led to give them.

One time, I did this in Burbank, California. I had been going on prayer walks during lunch breaks from work. I hesitate to give money to homeless people, fearing what they will do with the money. Personally, I'd rather buy them food. Sometimes, I've found that they'll refuse food because they only want money. I don't want to fund someone's addiction. Especially since often that is how they ended up on the streets.

One day, I walked around praying and saw a homeless lady on a bench near a bus stop. She had her various items — all she had left in the world — tucked into a shopping cart beside her.

I started to get that *sensation*. If you have ever felt it, you know the one. The one where you feel like God wants you to speak to a complete stranger. (This happens to a friend of mine often when she's in Walmart!) If you're anything like me, you may resist the impulse of the Holy Spirit the first time. You know. Because you want to be sure. Or, like me, you are a coward about talking to strangers.

I felt like I should approach the homeless woman to give her $20. I've never handed that much to one homeless person. It's usually just a few bucks or a $5 bill.

So I bargained with God. It went something like

this: "God, I'm going to walk around the block once. If she's still there, I will walk over to her and give her $20. But you know me and strangers. Help me talk to her."

There you have it. I told God I would. I walked around the block. The long way. (God probably laughed at me.)

Sure enough, she was still there when I got back to the bus stop. Suddenly, I felt God say to me, "Her name is Rose." I said, "Sure, right. I'm hearing ya." Yes, a bit sarcastically.

I really didn't think that was going to turn out to be true. I already knew in my heart I had committed to giving her the $20, regardless of her name simply because she was still there.

I walked over. Admittedly, I didn't have the guts to say, "Is your name Rose?" So instead, I asked her, "What's your name?"

In her gruff voice, she barked out, "Rose."

Imagine what it was like for me to then attempt to explain that God had just told me her name. From her point of view, it probably would have been more authentic if had I said, "Is your name Rose?" But from mine, it was far more likely to be confirmed if she gave me her name first. I knew, without a doubt, God spoke to me.

I, in my clunky way, attempted to explain God told me her name and told me to give her $20 as a gift from Him. She gladly took it and then accused homeless guy "Sam" from the bus stop down the street of telling me her name. She didn't believe me.

As I walked away, I prayed that God would get through to her. Convince her that He was the one who blessed her that day.

All we can do is plant seeds along the way. My prayer for you today is that you be open, give away what God tells you to. It could be to one person. It could be to many people or a group or family. Just go and take that leap of faith and see what He will guide you to do and what He will guide you to say to that person. If He leads you to pray with them or share an encouraging word, do it.

You never know what impact you could have on the life of another person who God loves as deeply as He loves you. You might just be the answer to their prayers.

Date 20
Power Prayers

Location: A quiet, private place.
Supplies: A willing heart.
Reading: Read chapter during your date.

This chapter is divided into two segments. There's one section for single women and another for those who are married.

The section for single women is excerpted from my book for singles, *Finally the Bride: Finding Hope While Waiting.* When I reposted this segment on my blog, calling it *16 Ways to Pray for Your Future Husband,* it quickly grew to the most popular blog on my *Finally One* website. Even all these years later since posting, I often still get over 100 readers a day.

Finally One is meant to be a site for married

people, a ministry my husband and I are building. And yet most of our readers have been single, hungry to find the loves of their lives.

This date is for one purpose: To pray for your spouse, whether you know that person yet or not.

Keeping that person in prayer should be a huge priority. Before and after marriage. Before and after that first date. I advocate dating after marriage (as long as it's your spouse, of course. Or God.)

This relationship should be as close to our relationship with God as any other. This includes romance, closeness, intimacy, love, and affection.

For Single Women
I will start with single women. If you are already married, skip ahead to that section of this same chapter and go through those prayers tailored to your husband.

Who you marry is one of the most important decisions you will ever make. It's an aspect of your life that is best navigated in full consultation with the heavenly Father of the bride.

Waiting can be a source of pain. I'd like to guide you through prayers for that future mate during this date with God. Honestly, I believe God cares more about your future marriage than you do. He would welcome the time with you — on a date with Him — to help you focus prayers in the right direction.

16 Ways to Pray for Your Future Husband

If anyone knows what's it's like to wait to find love and marriage, it's me. I waited 39 long years of life to walk down the aisle. Trusting God during the long wait was sometimes extremely difficult. Some days, all I could do was pray.

I started to realize that "all I could do" was actually quite significant. I found out later how God-led my prayers actually were, once God revealed to me who I was going to marry and what he was going through in his life when I chose to pray certain things. My prayers mattered; my prayers paid off. When waiting to find a husband and get married, it can seem like you are helpless and "doing nothing."

One of the best things to do while waiting is to pray for your future husband. To follow are 16 prayer points that you can focus on during your waiting season, to pray for his preparation.

You likely won't know who that person is going to be when you are praying these prayers. Thankfully, God does. And every prayer counts! (If you do happen to be dating the one you either think or know you are going to marry, feel free to adjust any of these prayer points as you deem appropriate to fit him.)

1. Pray for his walk with God, that he continues to grow spiritually and is

prepped to be the spiritual head of a household, and that he makes God the top priority in his life.

2. Pray for his ability to hear God's voice, for his ear to be in tune to hear all of God's instructions.

3. Pray for his will to be bendable toward whatever God wants for his life.

4. Pray for his emotional health — that any past wounds be dealt with and healed. Pray for restoration in all areas.

5. Pray for his physical health.

6. Pray that he breaks free of any unhealthy addictions, if needed.

7. Pray for his career, his life's work, that he be established in the field where God wants to use him and that he be wise with his resources.

8. Pray for his ministry — that he is sensitive to God's call on his life when it comes to ministering to and serving others. Also, pray for God to prepare both of you for the ways you will minister together.

9. Pray for his preparation — that he yields to all that God's potter's hands would like to accomplish in him.

10. Pray for God to send any trials necessary into his life that will allow the preparation process to be complete. I realize that may be a bit controversial. But knowing how much God has accomplished in my life through trials, I would expect nothing less of my husband's journey toward me.

11. Pray for God to prepare him to be a father, if the two of you will ultimately raise a family together.

12. Pray for God to help him be responsible with his finances and prepare him to be a significant contributor and provider to the household.

13. Pray for his identity as a man, his masculinity and self-esteem, that he grows into the man God wants him to be.

14. Pray for him to not be distracted by any counterfeits — especially other women that God doesn't intend to use for his growth.

15. Pray for God to allow this man to see you the way God wants you to be seen, with God's heart toward you.

16. Pray for God to show you how to

pray for your husband. Be open to whatever His Spirit may whisper to you, to cover your husband's needs. If you feel God gives you something specific, write it down and date it. Save it for later.

I hope that praying these prayers will encourage you in your waiting, and help you feel that you can accomplish much in the spiritual realm. I pray you will wait on God's best.

For Married Women

Okay, married women. Now it's your turn to pray for your husband. The husband you chose. The husband you promised to have and to hold, to honor and cherish, for better or worse, in sickness and in health, until death do you part.

The movie *War Room* shows in dramatized form how one woman helped change her husband, not by nagging, begging, pleading, correcting, or cajoling.

Instead, by *praying* for her husband.

She left the work up to God instead of leaving it up to herself to train him to be the husband that she needed. In his case, he was neglecting her and their daughter, and he was close to having an affair.

My husband and I happen to get along wonderfully, and I have never sought to change him. I rather like him just as he is. You can ask him as my witness. I don't nag him for anything. (He often compliments me on my restraint.)

I got my inspiration from my sister, Heather, watching her interact with her husband. I noticed even when it felt like she had the right to nag, she chose not to. She demonstrated this so well for me long before I got married.

One thing our husbands need from us is our prayers, not our laundry list of suggestions for them. Ways to change. Things to do. Methods to improve. They need what God can provide for them.

So on this date, I want you to invite God into your relationship with your spouse. Invite Him to lead your prayers. He may be a jealous God; He may want your attention. But He also is the world's biggest champion of marriage.

God created marriage. He created sex. He created this "institution" as a symbol of greater things to come when Christ returns for His church, The Bride. I am so thankful God gave us this slice of heaven on earth.

So, now, for your date. Let's get praying. I'll include a prayer guide for you here to direct you. Feel free to veer off to specifics that you know about your husband and needs that may be going on in his life right now. You can even ask God to direct you in praying for your husband. God knows him better than you do.

1. Pray for your husband's physical health.

2. Pray for your husband's emotional health. You can pinpoint areas that concern you or pray for continued health if you feel he is steady in this area.

3. Pray for your husband's spiritual health, that he feel drawn to spend time alone with God and time in prayer with you. Pray for him to have sensitivity to hear God's voice and direction for himself and to lead your family.

4. Pray for his career path, his fulfillment in it, or any changes that may need to take place for him so he's more creatively challenged, if need be.

5. Pray for his unfulfilled dreams. You probably know better than most the dreams on his heart that haven't come to pass. Pray for those. Care about those. Pray regarding how you could help him realize those dreams (but without taking over). Pray for God to show you if there are any sacrifices you can make in order to help see them come to fruition. (Ex.

Allowing time and money for schooling, taking on more of the household management to give him time to pursue his dream.)

6. Pray for his role as father, if he currently is one, or for his future as a parent if he is not one yet and you hope or plan to be parents. Pray for him to have biblical wisdom in raising children.

7. Pray that your husband not be distracted by other people, other women, and other priorities that are not good for your marriage.

8. Pray for him to not succumb to any past addictions or develop unhealthy new ones.

9. Pray for his love for you to grow every day, his bond and connection with you — physically, emotionally.

10. If there is anything in particular you need from your husband but haven't been able to ask, now is a great time to ask God to help take care of that. Either Himself or through your husband. Pray for God to help rather than you having to resort to nagging or continuous reminding.

11. Pray for his daily protection during his comings and goings.

12. Pray for his self-esteem. As a man, a husband, a father, one who is contributing meaningfully to your lives and at work.

13. Pray for him to exhibit fruit of the Spirit. Ask God to strengthen him against the fruit of the flesh.

14. Pray for him to be able to become all that he is meant to be in the Lord. To fulfill every calling that God has in mind for him.

15. Pray for him to be the spouse that God has intended for you. God's heart is for you and it's for your husband, too. We're all humans and make mistakes. Pray for both of you to become who you are meant to be for each other, if that's not happening already. Ask God to highlight areas for you to improve, if needed. (Don't be afraid to ask that question. It will only make your life and marriage better.)

16. Pray for God to fill you with a love for your husband, and help you see your husband the way God sees him.

Those prayer lists are not exhaustive. Whether you are single or married, feel free to add whatever prayers God puts on your heart for your future spouse or your husband.

God is happy to be invited into the process of your prayers for this most special and important man in your life.

Date 21
Writing a Love Song

Location: A quiet place.

Supplies: A journal, a musical instrument if you play
   one, manuscript paper if you write music.

Reading: Read chapter during your date.

As mentioned, in 2003, when I was in the darkest
depression of my life, I started the tradition of
"Prayer Walks." Occasionally I'd sing praise songs
I'd learned in church. A few months into my
tradition of hanging out with God this way, a song
started to emerge in my heart. The lyrics, the tune.

   I wanted to remember it, so I recorded it. Still to
this day, well over 10 years later, I find myself
humming this special tune that God put on my heart
all those years ago during a difficult time.

Psalm 40:3 says, "He put a new song in my mouth, a hymn of praise to our God. Many will see and fear the LORD and put their trust in Him."

He put a new song in my mouth.

That's what God did for me. My praise song — let's just say it's very basic. Repetitive. I am not a songwriter. Never plan to be. But this song is mine and God's together. A song I sang during a tough time, to show Him I still loved Him, that I'd still walk with Him no matter what.

The lyric about walking was no accident since I was always singing this out on prayer walks. I'd like to share with you the lyrics. (Thankfully, you don't have to hear me sing it.)

> "You are the Lord, you are worthy of praise / You are my God over all of my days / I walk with You each step of the way / I walk with You each step of the way / I walk with You each step of the way / I will follow You all of my days / I will follow You all of my days."

Yes, there's repetition. This became my theme song during my eight-month depression. A reminder to God and me that I wasn't going to leave Him, to walk away, to reject Him because of the pain He'd allowed into my life.

In fact, it was during this time He'd spoken to

my heart and said that a small amount of pain now would save me from a lot of pain later. I knew He meant it. I knew what He was talking about. It didn't feel like a "small amount of pain" to me at the time. But I knew He was telling me that if I had married the man I was dating, we'd be divorced years down the road. Breaking up before we got engaged was far less painful than what could have been. God was protecting me from pain, even if not 100 percent. That song was birthed out of pain.

Now it's your turn. You may not be able to sing; you may not be able to write. That is not a requirement here. Feel free to rap a song if you can't carry a tune.

Ask God: Does He have a song lyric to put on your heart? Does He have a theme He wants you to sing to Him? Has that already begun on a prior date? If so, no problem. Write it down if you haven't already. Record the tune or rap.

Ask Him to "put a new song in your mouth" and see what He will do. I never prayed that prayer at the time. He just did this on His own. But I needed a new song on my heart. And He delivered.

God loves to be praised. I have no doubt He'll offer this to you as well if you take the time to open your heart (and mouth) to Him.

After all, this is just like a lover asking you to write a song for them. (My husband, Chris, has written at least seven songs for me thus far. I find it romantic.) Why not do the same for the God who is the Lover of your soul?

Date 22
All About Faith

Location: A quiet place.
Supplies: A journal.
Reading: Read chapter during your date.

$\mathcal{H}$ave you ever taken one of those spiritual gifts tests that help you discern what you're good at? They normally extract the gifts from Romans 12:3-8 and 1 Corinthians 12, and ask you questions that are all derived from behaviors tied to those gifts. You score yourself after to determine your strengths or strongest gifts, and the areas that you aren't so great at. Here are portions from each chapter:

> Romans 12:3-8
> "For by the grace given me I say to every

one of you: Do not think of yourself more highly than you ought, but rather think of yourself with sober judgment, in accordance with the faith God has distributed to each of you. 4 For just as each of us has one body with many members, and these members do not all have the same function, 5 so in Christ we, though many, form one body, and each member belongs to all the others. 6 We have different gifts, according to the grace given to each of us. If your gift is prophesying, then prophesy in accordance with your faith; 7 if it is serving, then serve; if it is teaching, then teach; 8 if it is to encourage, then give encouragement; if it is giving, then give generously; if it is to lead, do it diligently; if it is to show mercy, do it cheerfully."

I'll quote a portion of 1 Corinthians 12, but the whole chapter is worth reading:

1 Corinthians 12:7-11
"Now to each one the manifestation of the Spirit is given for the common good. 8 To one there is given through the Spirit a message of wisdom, to another a message of knowledge by means of the same Spirit, 9 to another faith by the same Spirit, to another

> gifts of healing by that one Spirit, 10 to another miraculous powers, to another prophecy, to another distinguishing between spirits, to another speaking in different kinds of tongues, and to still another the interpretation of tongues. 11 All these are the work of one and the same Spirit, and He distributes them to each one, just as He determines."

In a future installment of this book series, we'll explore more about those gifts. But this chapter will focus on the one that is this book's theme: faith. Most often when I've taken those tests, I've scored off the charts on the *gift of faith*.

I have this problem: I believe God.

Sometimes, this causes me pain, especially when He makes a promise then waits till Kingdom Come (so it seems) to fulfill it. Someone with the gift of faith has a special ability to believe for the impossible.

Because it's one of my strongest gifts, it's also where I am targeted by the enemy. He'd like nothing more than to convince me that God can't be trusted or God isn't going to do what He says. Satan wants me to give up. To speak negative words about what God won't do or especially who God is (or isn't). Whether those promises are written directly in the Word of God or on my heart through conversations we've had, Satan loves to attack them. He absolutely does not want me to believe God. He probably knows he can't get me to not believe *in* God. But the enemy would sure like to convince me that God is not trustworthy and drive a wedge between us.

Since this installment of *Dates With God* is called *Adventures in Faith*, I wanted to include one date that gives you the opportunity to meditate on verses about our *faith*, our *faithful* God, and *trust*.

Remember: Going on dates with God during this season of your life takes faith. You trust there is a real God, that He wants to spend time with you, and that He will show up on these dates. Even though He's omnipresent and always with you, there is something different about when He tangibly shows up on a date with His daughters.

So let this particular date be about building your trust in God. Trust is the benchmark of a strong relationship. Marriages thrive when faith, faithfulness and trust are there. Why not also make sure those traits are hallmarks of your relationship with God?

So, what are you waiting for? Take time now to ponder these verses on our faith, our faithful God, and trust.

Our Faith

Hebrews 11:1
"Now faith is confidence in what we hope for and assurance about what we do not see."

Hebrews 11:6
"And without faith it is impossible to please God, because anyone who comes to Him must believe that He exists and that He rewards those who earnestly seek Him."

2 Corinthians 5:7
"For we live by faith, not by sight."

Galatians 2:20
"I have been crucified with Christ and I no longer live, but Christ lives in me. The life I now live in the body, I live by faith in the Son of God, who loved me and gave Himself for me."

1 Corinthians 16:13
"Be on your guard; stand firm in the faith; be courageous; be strong."

Romans 5:1
"Therefore, since we have been justified

through faith, we have peace with God through our LORD Jesus Christ."

2 Chronicles 20:20b
"Have faith in the LORD your God and you will be upheld."

Our Faithful God

Psalm 33:4
"For the word of the LORD is right and true; He is faithful in all He does."

Psalm 145:13b
"...The LORD is trustworthy in all His promises and faithful in all He does."

1 Corinthians 1:9
"God is faithful, who has called you into fellowship with His Son, Jesus Christ our Lord."

1 Thessalonians 5:24a
"The One who calls you is faithful..."

2 Thessalonians 3:3
"But the LORD is faithful, and He will strengthen you and protect you from the evil one."

Hebrews 10:23
"Let us hold unswervingly to the hope we profess, for He who promised is faithful."

Trust

Psalm 9:10
"Those who know Your name trust in You, for You, LORD, have never forsaken those who seek You."

Psalm 20:7
"Some trust in chariots and some in horses, but we trust in the name of the LORD our God."

Psalm 22:4
"In You our ancestors put their trust; they trusted and You delivered them."

Psalm 25:2

"I trust in You; do not let me be put to shame, nor let my enemies triumph over me."

Psalm 31:14

"But I trust in You, LORD; I say, 'You are my God.'"

Psalm 33:21

"In Him our hearts rejoice, for we trust in His holy name."

Psalm 37:3

"Trust in the LORD and do good; dwell in the land and enjoy safe pasture."

Psalm 37:5a

"Commit your way to the LORD; trust in Him..."

Psalm 52:8b

"I trust in God's unfailing love forever and ever."

Psalm 56:3

"When I am afraid, I put my trust in You."

Psalm 56:11

"In God I trust and am not afraid. What can man do to me?"

Psalm 62:8

"Trust in Him at all times, you people; pour out your hearts to Him, for God is our refuge."

Psalm 91:2

"I will say of the LORD, 'He is my refuge and my fortress, my God, in whom I trust.'"

Psalm 115:11

"You who fear Him, trust in the LORD — He is their help and shield."

Psalm 143:8

"Let the morning bring me word of Your unfailing love, for I have put my trust in You. Show me the way I should go, for to You I entrust my life."

Proverbs 3:5–6

"Trust in the LORD with all your heart and lean not on your own understanding; in all your ways submit to Him, and He will make your paths straight."

Proverbs 29:25

"Fear of man will prove to be a snare, but whoever trusts in the LORD is kept safe."

Isaiah 12:2

"Surely God is my salvation; I will trust and not be afraid. The LORD, the LORD Himself is my strength and my defense; He has become my salvation."

Isaiah 26:4

"Trust in the LORD forever, for the LORD, the LORD Himself, is the Rock eternal."

Jeremiah 39:18

"'I will save you; you will not fall by the sword but will escape with your life, because you trust in Me,'" declares the LORD."

Nahum 1:7

"The LORD is good, a refuge in times of trouble. He cares for those who trust in Him."

I love that verse in Hebrews that reminds us, *"He who promised is faithful."* Another verse I'd like to highlight feels like a "benchmark verse" for all of our dates with God:

> 1 Peter 1:8-9
> "Though you have not seen Him, you love Him; and even though you do not see Him now, you believe in Him and are filled with an inexpressible and glorious joy, for you are receiving the end result of your faith, the salvation of your souls."

Isn't that an awesome sentiment to go into every date from here on forward? You may not see Him "in the natural" with your physical eyes. But by faith, you see Him with your spiritual eyes.

You love Him. Maybe you're even falling more in love with Him with every date, just like an earthly relationship should grow after each date. Especially as you get to know that person on a deeper level, including after marriage. I'm always learning new things about my husband. That just naturally comes with time spent together.

The more time you spend with God, the more you will know Him. The more you will love Him.

The more your faith in Him will grow.

Date 23
Reader's Choice

Location: Your choice.
Supplies: Your choice.
Reading: Read whole chapter before your date.

*H*as this first installment of the *Dates With God* series given you ideas for dates with God that I haven't suggested? When you've been out on other dates, has your mind been sparked with creative ideas for other dates? Now is the time to go on one of those.

First, start a journal entry to write down a list of ideas of other things you'd like to do with God. What are your unique interests, talents, and hobbies that you could put into action on a date?

For example, do you want to go on a picnic date

with God while out kayaking?

Do you have a particular hobby that you'd enjoy alone with God? For example, geocaching. If you are a geocacher, would you like to hide a little canister with something Bible related for others to find? Then post the GPS coordinates online.

Are you an accomplished rock climber? Of course that activity is best spent with a buddy. Take someone with you on this double date who may be able to use some intimate time with God as well. Have some planned prayer time when you arrive at the top. Maybe use the Bible on your phone.

I'm not designing specific dates around these sample activities since many may not know how to do these or have access to resources needed. However, I want to give you a chance to stop, think about your areas of interest and resources, and have you turn those into dates.

Brainstorm now. Write a list. Even though this is just one date you'll go on now, why not save ideas for future dates too? Once you finish a list, pick one of those to do now.

While I plan at least four volumes of this book series, plus a special Holiday Edition, I welcome you to add your own creativity into this divine dating relationship.

Design your own creative date. Go on it, take selfies and then, if you're willing, post about it with the #dateswithGod label on social media, like

Twitter or Instagram. (If you use Twitter you can tag us at @purplepenworks.) You can also go to our website, **www.dateswithGod.com**, and leave a comment on the page for Volume One of this series.

Feel free to just share your experience in a comment, or give us a link to where you've either blogged about your date or posted photos. By doing so, you will encourage others who are also "dating God" to have even more fun than they've had so far by following my guided ideas. I don't pretend to be able to come up with every idea under the sun that we could enjoy on dates with God. So I really want to welcome you into this process.

I plan to publish segments of Reader's Choice *Dates With God*. So if you're willing to share your ideas, please do so. Maybe your date will be the one that will change someone's relationship with God for the better. If God has met you in a special way on a date unique to you, we'd love to hear your testimony.

So, that's it. Easy enough, right? Write that list and take your first date from your list of ideas. In the future, revisit that list and try them all at least once. Repeat your favorites.

And share with us how it goes!

Date 24
Scrapbooking Your Dates

Location: A place at home with a large table or desk.
Supplies: A journal, your camera, computer, pictures
from your dates, a scrapbook and supplies, or an
online scrapbooking program.
Reading: Read whole chapter before your date.

We are getting close to the end of this first volume.
Don't worry. If this has been an enjoyable process for
you, this is just Volume One and there will be more.
I believe we should be dating God for the rest of our
lives.

Even working on this project, I've asked God a
few times: "What date would you like to go on
today?" I know with His vast wealth of creativity,
He will always supply new, fun ideas. Intimate

ideas, faith-building ideas.

Before you get to the final date, where you will do a relationship check-in with God, I'd like you to use this date as a "look back" on all the dates you've been on so far. I've encouraged you along the way to take pictures. Pictures of things He's shown you, pictures of His beautiful artistry in nature, GodWinks, selfies of you on dates. Gather all of these pictures. Now it's time to put them together in some form of a scrapbook. This date may take a few days or a week or so because it is a project.

There are various approaches to this date you can take. You can choose to scrapbook your dates in a real live scrapbook with stickers and decorations. You can use a journaling photo album. You can start a blog about your dates, complete with photos. Or you can put together an online scrapbook.

I am an avid scrapbooker. The paper kind. For years now, my mom, my sister, and I have built scrapbooks of our lives. I tend to like them in print. Scrapbooking on a computer feels too much like work to me since I work on a computer all day. However, I understand if you'd like to lessen your cost and carbon footprint and just enjoy your memories online or on your computer.

Allow me to go into a bit more detail about each approach.

You can go as far as building a *Dates With God* scrapbook, on paper. What a faith-building book that would be to go through! It could even be an interesting conversation starter when you have friends over. If you want to do that, buy supplies and order prints of photos in advance of this date. Get theme stickers that fit the dates you took and any other décor you'd like.

Another method would be to buy a journal style photo album that has room to write notes beside each photo instead of making a full scrapbook. It should leave room for each photo, plus a place to write up your story. (Don't forget to journal about any GodWink pictures!)

You could also start a blog about this experience, writing entries about various dates with pictures included. What fun to share your stories, testimonials about how God showed up, complete with photo proof. You can be part of this whole *Dates With God* movement.

The online scrapbook version could be just for you. They make programs you can use to save pictures and stories electronically. Like I said, for me this is too much like work. I prefer the photo or scrapbook album method myself. But being one who lost all photo albums and journals and scrapbooks once to toxic mold, there's definitely value in electronically stored entries.

This project will chronicle all the time you've spent with God since this journey began. Once you choose your method for scrapbooking, label your photos with what date number they were from out of this book, if you haven't already.

Next, look up things in your journal that God said to you on each date. Pick out a special quote or piece of wisdom you feel He showed you on each date that goes with the pictures. Just like the *Milestones with God* assignment, this can be a faith builder.

By now, you have probably had 23 new experiences with God that you haven't had before. Save them and capture those memories.

Like any dating relationship, looking back on where we've been and the good times we've had is a fun activity. Especially if you've built good memories together. This date helps you do this visually. The next date will get into having some concentrated chat time with God to check in on your relationship.

Meanwhile, as you work through this project, I hope you enjoy your trip down memory lane.

Date 25
Relationship Check-In

Location: A quiet place.
Supplies: A journal.
Reading: Read chapter during your date.

Congrats on making it this far, all the way to Date 25. I look forward to having you join me again for dates in future volumes of this book series. The possibilities of dating God are endless.

For this date, choose any location, perhaps even your favorite location from Dates 1-24. It's time to do one of those "relationship check-ins." You know the kind.

The "Where are we in this relationship" or "State of the Union" conversation.

Sometimes—in dating—those talks could be

scary, especially if both parties weren't on the same page. (I had more than one of those when dating men before Chris. Not so fun.)

I can promise you that if you've been participating actively in these dates, your relationship is stronger than it was 24 dates ago. You've probably grown, gotten to know more about God, His wonderful attributes, His personality, and His love for you. My hope is your love for Him is exponentially higher. But it always helps to stop, take inventory, and check-in.

You don't have to feel any of those awkward jitters in your stomach. God already loves and accepts you. He is more than happy to come to the table to chat with you. He wants a good relationship with you even more than you do. He's not about to tell you it's over.

As you settle into your comfortable place, open the journal you started at the beginning of this dating relationship.

Go back to the journal entry for Date 1. What did you write in answer to the questions posed for that date? I want you to reread it now so you can reflect in your journal about what has changed.

- Do you feel closer to God than you did before?
- Do you feel like you know God better?
- What was your favorite date of the 24 thus far

-191-

and why? Are there any you would like to
repeat?

- What was your least favorite and why? Is it
worth doing over?
- In what ways did God show up on dates for
you during this time that you hadn't
experienced before?
- What are your future goals regarding your
relationship with God?
- Make a plan: How would you like your
dating relationship with God to continue?
- Did you learn anything new about God that
you didn't know before? Anything that
surprised you?

Next, ask God a few questions and jot down
anything you feel He says to you:

- God, how do you feel about our relationship
now versus before?
- Have I grown?
- Where can I improve in my quest to know
You better, Lord?
- Have I let anything come between You and
me since our original "inventory" prayer
asking for forgiveness of my sins?
- What kinds of dates would You like to go on

with me in the future?

- Is there anything I'm not asking that You'd like to share with me?

Make a plan and schedule to keep going after you close this book. Naturally, you can always reread and revisit the dates in this book. I want to make sure this is an ongoing thing for you. It doesn't end here with Date 25.

The goal of this book is to help you establish a continuous relationship. I don't want you to finish this book and stop dating God. If anything, I want this book to have ignited a passion in you for Him, to kindle the flame that makes you want to go back to God over and over for these special dates.

Hopefully, this check-in results in that mutual decision to keep dating. To continue the relationship and not end it here because it's "just not working out." We've all been there, right? But God is not going to reject you. He craves relationship with you. He will not come to this table and say, "You know what? It's over. We're just not compatible."

This part is *your* decision. Will you stay in this relationship? Will you continue to play a huge role in how much it grows?

You are safe, you are accepted, and you are

loved and wanted. You are not abandoned by Him. This is the safest dating relationship you can ever be in. He will never leave you. Not even death can separate you from your True Love.

God is inviting you into a dance, a life long dating relationship that never has to end, even in death.

So open your hand, accept His in yours, and enjoy a romance that can only be written by God.

About the Author

Cheryl McKay has been professionally writing since 1997. Tommy Nelson was her first publisher, teaming her with Frank Peretti on the *Wild and Wacky, Totally True Bible Stories* series. Cheryl wrote the screenplay adaptation of *The Ultimate Gift*, the feature film starring Academy Award Nominees James Garner and Abigail Breslin. It's based on Jim Stovall's best-selling novel. The film was released by Fox in theaters in Spring 2007 and has won such awards as the Crystal Heart Award, the Crystal Dove, one of the Top Ten Family Movies at MovieGuide Awards, and a CAMIE Award. She also wrote the DVD for *Gigi: God's Little Princess*, another book adaptation based on the book by Sheila Walsh, and episodes of *Superbook*. She wrote a half-hour drama for teenagers about high school violence, called *Taylor's Wall*, produced in Los Angeles by Family Theater

Productions. After winning a fellowship, she was commissioned to write a feature script, *Greetings from the Flipside,* for Art Within, which Rene Gutteridge and McKay released as a novel through B&H Publishing in October 2013. Her screenplay, *Never the Bride,* was adapted into a novel by Gutteridge and was released by Waterbrook Press in June 2009. The film version is in development. As one passionate for those who are losing hope in their wait to find love, she released the nonfiction version, *Finally the Bride: Finding Hope While Waiting.* She also penned her autobiography, *Finally Fearless: Journey from Panic to Peace.* She wrote the screen story for *The Ultimate Life,* the sequel to *The Ultimate Gift.* In the future, look for films *Extraordinary* and *Indivisible,* both faith-based features co-written by McKay. Find her on Facebook, Twitter, Pinterest, or at her websites:

www.purplepenworks.com
www.finallyone.com
www.dateswithGod.com

$\mathcal{D}$ear Readers:

Thank you for spending this time with me and more importantly with the God who loves you so much. I hope you will join me for future installments of this book series and take more dates with God.

If this book has been helpful to you, please recommend it to your friends and family. Would you mind leaving a review online where you purchased this book to share your thoughts with others?

Also, please visit our website and share your date experiences: **www.dateswithGod.com**.

I wish you many blessings in your quest to know your loving Heavenly Father deeper and wider and more intimately.

Blessings,

Cheryl McKay

Dates With God **Series:**

Volume One: *Adventures in Faith*
Volume Two: *Courting Spiritual Intimacy*
Volume Three: *Falling in Love with Jesus*
Volume Four: *Pursuing the Lover of Your Soul*

Holiday Edition: Love Worth Celebrating

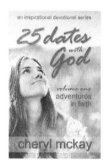

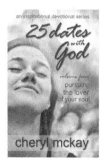

Finally the Bride

Finding Hope While Waiting

Cheryl McKay

Finally Fearless

Journey from Panic to Peace

How Overcoming
Anxiety Helped Me
Find True Love

cheryl mckay

Other Books by the Author

Made in the USA
Columbia, SC
25 July 2021

42381322R00111